Air Law for Microlight

Air Law for Microlight Pilots

Aviation Law for Microlights and all forms of Sport Flying

Geoff Weighell

ISBN 987 1 874783 794

Published by

AFE

Airplan Flight Equipment Ltd

This book is intended to be a guide to the Aviation Law element of the UK NPPL(M) course. It **does not** in any way overrule the instruction you will receive from a suitably qualified Instructor at a registered training facility. No part of this book overrules or supersedes the Air Navigation Order (ANO), the Aeronautical Information Publication (AIP), Aeronautical Information Circulars (AIC), the Joint Aviation Requirements (JAR) and other documents published by a competent authority. Nor does it overrule or supersede the flight manual/manufacturer's operating handbook for the aircraft being flown, the pilot order book/flying training syllabus and the general provisions of good airmanship and safe flying practice. Aviation rules and regulations change on a regular basis, at the back of this book there is a recommended reading list of official aviation documents.

First Edition 2007

Air Law for Microlight Pilots
Aviation Law for Microlights and all forms of Sport Flying

ISBN 978 1 874783 794

Airplan Flight Equipment Ltd
1a Ringway Trading Estate, Shadowmoss Road, Manchester M22 5LH
Tel: 0161 499 0023 Fax: 0161 499 0298
email: enquiries@afeonline.com
www.afeonline.com

Contents

Editorial

AUTHOR: Geoff Weighell

Geoff Weighell started flying in the mid 1970's, learning to fly hang gliders at the Dunstable School of Hang Gliding. With the development of power units that could be fitted to hang gliders offering a wider window of flying conditions a move to flying microlights was natural. There were no dual seat aircraft at the time and so Geoff took to the skies with some advice and lots of hope.

In 1983 Geoff became a microlight instructor and began to teach pilots to fly in the new two seat aircraft. Starting his own school at Enstone in Oxfordshire in 1986 Geoff continued to teach as a full time occupation until late in 2006.

Geoff's interests in flying have also included competition flying in microlights. He was British Champion in 1986 and a member of the British Microlight team that won the first World Microlight Championships in 1985. In 2003 Geoff started flying helicopters and competed as crewman in three British Championships and one World Championship.

As well as flying microlights Geoff has taken an active role in administration of the microlight instruction system. He has been Chairman of the Microlight Panel of Examiners and the British Microlight Aircraft Association (BMAA). He was deeply involved with the development of the National Private Pilot's Licence and is still a part of the steering group that oversees the running of that licence system.

In the Autumn of 2006 Geoff joined the BMAA as Chief Executive and now has a full time role helping to administer the sport of microlight flying in the UK. He still holds and instructor rating and continues to instruct part time and fly for pleasure whenever possible.

Acknowledgments

This book would also not have been possible without the assistance of the following people and organisations:

Keith Negal

Jeremy M Pratt, AFE

Colin Taylor

Robert Taylor, GDi studio

Introduction

Aviation Law is often seen as the least interesting of the subjects studied during training to become a pilot, it is however a very important one. Aviation Law exists to regulate the safety of all airspace users of all types of aircraft included in which, of course, is you in your aircraft.

This book sets out to detail those parts of Aviation Law which are relevant to sports aviation (recreational) pilots, focusing on microlight pilots where powered aircraft are concerned, and to explain the detail in a commonsense way which I hope will help you learn. Try to think of how each topic will practically affect the way you operate your aircraft, this will help you to remember relevant detail.

There have been changes to the detail of air legislation over the years and no doubt there will be changes in the future. No book will remain accurate for very long so you should keep aware of changes which may occur by reading the publications published by the UK Civil Aviation Authority and their agents. You will find a list of documents used for reference at the end of this book together with contact addresses for information on the topics covered.

Try to enjoy this subject, it will be easier to learn if you can and a better knowledge will help to keep you flying safely for a long time to come.

Geoff Weighell

Spring 2007

Key: Where a subject or regulation applies to a particular type of aircraft, or is just good airmanship irrespective of type, it will be highlighted with a symbol as below:

Microlight 

Powered Parachute 

Foot Launched Powered Flying Machine or Self Propelled Hang Glider 

Glider 

Hang Glider 

Paraglider 

Gyroplane 

Balloon 

Aviation Legislation

▶ Aviation Legislation

▶ Aviation Legislation

The basis of United Kingdom aviation law is an agreement between the member states of the International Civil Aviation Organisation (ICAO) following a Convention held in Chicago in 1944. The agreement seeks to standardise legislation for safety and regulatory purposes.

United Kingdom aviation law results from this Convention and an Act of Parliament details the regulations which resulted. The Civil Aviation Authority is the body responsible for overseeing the implementation of the regulations.

The United Kingdom is also subject to legislation produced by the European Union. The EU has formed an agency, the European Aviation Safety Agency (EASA), which is required to promote aviation safety by regulating aviation operating procedures throughout the EU. The intention is to require uniform standards across the member States of the EU to achieve the framework for safe flight operations. At the time of writing, EASA is mainly concerned with airworthiness issues and has chosen initially to exempt many of the aircraft flown by recreational pilots. The aircraft exempted are listed at ANNEX 11 of EC Regulation 1592/2002.

The EASA is also concerned with pilot licensing standardisation and it can be expected that in the future its recommendations will impinge on the UK requirements although at present they do not do so.

The precise details of the regulations to which we are subject are included in several large volumes which have been used as reference for this guide. Full details of the regulations can be found in the actual documents which are referred to throughout this text. Actual reference details may change from time to time but it is hoped that this guide will be as up to date and correct as possible.

As you are studying this document during your training to become a sports aviation pilot only the parts of Aviation Law which apply to you are included in this guide. If you wish to fly other categories of aircraft in the future you may have to study additional regulations that may apply.

European Aviation Safety Agency
(EASA)

European Union
(EU)

Aeronautical Information

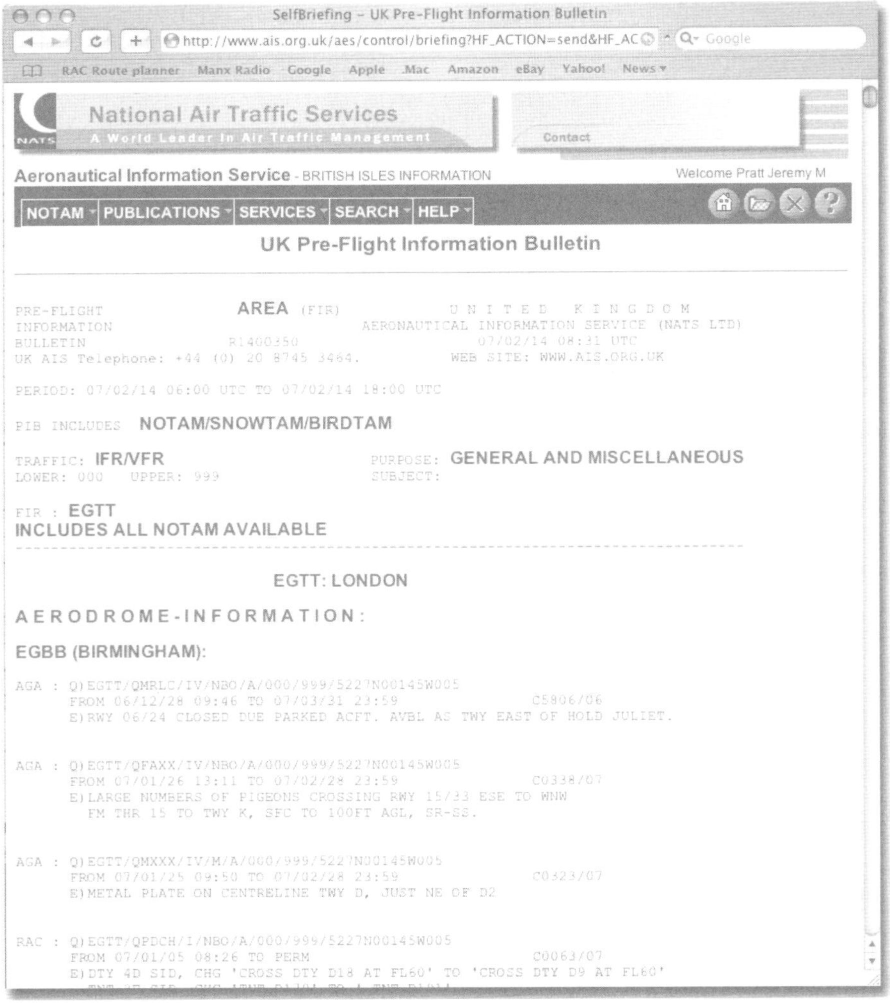

Aeronautical Information

- Aeronautical Information Service (AIS)
- Aeronautical Information Publication (AIP)
- Notices To Airmen, NOTAM
- Aeronautical Information Circulars (AIC)
- Pre-Flight Information Bulletins (PIB)
- Air Navigation Order (ANO)
- Revision

▶ Aeronautical Information Service (AIS)

The function of the AIS is to collect, collate, edit and disseminate the information necessary for safe and efficient air navigation to interested parties, including Air Traffic Control (ATC) services, flight crew and other aviation organisations.

Aeronautical information is published as an integrated package consisting of a number of elements.

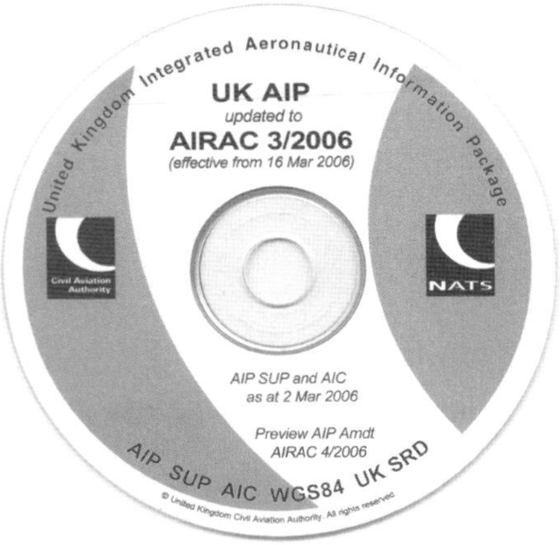

The AIP is available in hard copy, CD-Rom and via the AIS website

▶ Aeronautical Information Publication (AIP)

The Aeronautical Information Publication (AIP), including amendment services, is published in sections grouped as follows:

GEN (General) contains the following sections and detail:

GEN 1 National regulations and requirements – Designated authorities; Entry, transit and departure of aircraft, passengers and crew; Entry, transit and departure of cargo; Aircraft instruments, equipment and flight documents; Summary of navigation regulations and international agreements/conventions; Differences from ICAO Standards, Recommended Practices and Procedures.

GEN 2 Tables and Codes – Measuring systems, aircraft markings, holidays; Abbreviations used in AIS publications; Chart symbols; Location indicators; List of radio navigation aids; Conversion tables; Sunrise/Sunset tables; Climb gradient table.

GEN 3 Services – Aeronautical Information Services; Aeronautical charts; Air Traffic Services; Communications services; Meteorological services; Search and rescue.

GEN 4 Charges for aerodrome/heliport and air navigation services – Aerodrome/heliport charges; Air navigation service charges.

ENR (En-Route) contains the following parts and detail:

ENR 1 General rules and procedures – General rules; Visual flight rules (including of Special VFR flight); Instrument flight rules; ATS airspace classification; Holding, approach and departure procedures; Radar services and procedures; Altimeter setting procedures; Regional supplementary procedures; Air traffic flow management; Flight planning; Addressing of flight plan messages; Interception of civil aircraft; Unlawful interference; Air traffic incidents; Off-shore operations.

ENR 2 Air traffic services airspace – Detailed description of Flight Information Regions (FIR); Upper Flight Information Regions (UIR); Control Areas (CTA); Terminal Control Areas (TMA); Other regulated airspace.

ENR 3 ATS routes – Detailed description of Lower ATS routes; Upper ATS routes; Area Navigation routes; Helicopter routes; Other routes – Supersonic transport routes; En-route holding.

ENR 4 Radio navigation aids/systems – Radio navigation aids – en-route; Special navigation systems; Name-code designators for significant points; Aeronautical ground lights – en-route.

ENR 5 Navigation warnings – Prohibited, restricted and danger areas; Military exercise and training areas; Other activities of a dangerous nature; Air navigation obstacles – en-route; Aerial sporting and recreational activities; Bird migration and areas of sensitive fauna.

ENR 6 En-route charts – En-route Chart – ICAO and index charts.

AD (Aerodromes) contains the following parts and detail:

AD 1 Aerodromes/Heliports – Introduction – Aerodrome/heliport availability; Rescue and fire fighting services and snow plan; Index to aerodromes and heliports; Grouping of aerodromes and heliports.

AD 2 Aerodromes – Detailed information about civil licensed aerodromes published in the UK AIP (including RAF Northolt) and helicopter landing areas if located at the aerodromes.

AD 3 Heliports – Detailed information about civil licensed heliports published in the UK AIP (not located at aerodromes).

AIP Supplements are issued every 28 days containing temporary information.

Whilst much of the information in the AIP will never be used by the private pilot it is good to know where the detail may be found. It is usual for Clubs and Schools to have a copy of the AIP and for members to share it.

Most sections of the AIP are also available to view at the official AIS website. The address is: **www.ais.org.uk**

▶ Notices To Airmen, NOTAM

Notices To Airmen, NOTAM, contain temporary information which may affect the flight you are planning to make. Detail of activities such as airshows, kite flying, balloon festivals are common inclusions in NOTAM. Knowing about events and activities at sites other than aerodromes can help you to plan a safe route. Other information may relate to aerodrome availability. There are times when aerodromes may be closed for maintenance or non flying activities such as car rallies or, increasingly, outdoor markets. It is always better to find out that your planned destination, or fuel stop, is closed before you set out rather then when you arrive.

NOTAM are distributed through the Aeronautical Fixed Telecommunications Network, AFTN, to aerodromes subscribing to the service and are available to the private pilot through the AIS web site: **www.ais.org.uk**

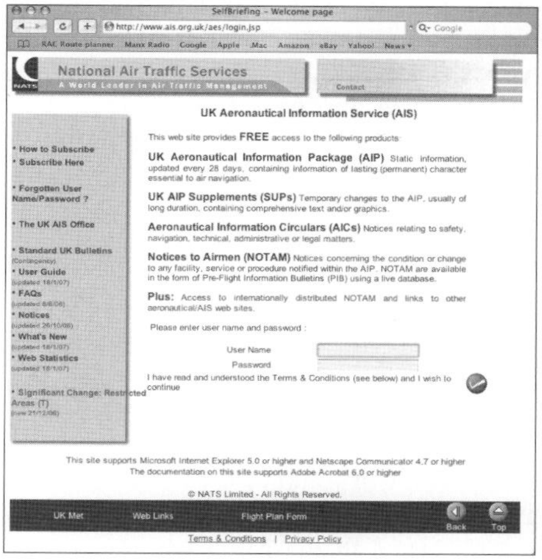

www.ais.org.uk

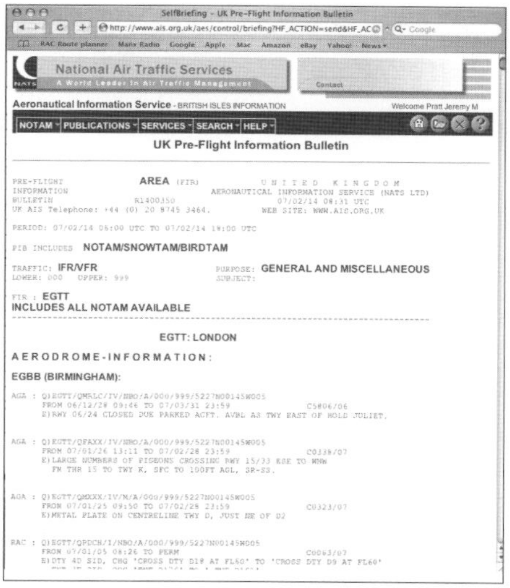

NOTAM information via the AIS website

▶ Aeronautical Information Circulars (AIC)

Aeronautical Information Circulars (AIC) are originated by the Civil Aviation Authority (CAA) and distributed by the AIS. Most of the subjects are administrative but some call attention to matters of operational importance and offer important safety advice. AIC are categorised by different colours according to their subject, as follows:

White	Administrative matters eg examination dates, charges.
Yellow	Operational matters including ATC services and requirements.
Pink	Matters of special importance to air safety.
Mauve	Amendments to UK airspace restriction charts (danger area map and military low flying map).
Green	Availability of CAA maps and charts.

Aeronautical Information Circulars

Unless revoked or replaced, AIC normally have a life of five years at which point they may be updated and re-issued.

Subscribers can receive 'hard copy' AIC every four weeks. AIC are also published on the AIS web site.

Unlike the AIP, AIC tend to have much more information relevant directly to the private pilot and I recommend that all pilots should try to check the content of each monthly batch as it is published.

▶ Pre-Flight Information Bulletins (PIB)

Pre-Flight Information Bulletins (PIB) are an addition to the integrated package and include General, Aerodrome and Navigation Warning Bulletins issued to subscribers twice weekly. The content varies but will include such activities as kite flying, air displays, air races etc.

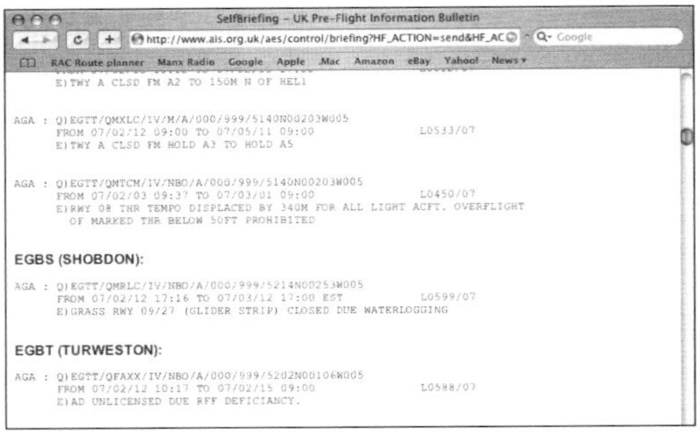

A sample pre-flight information bulletin showing various temporary hazards

▶ Air Navigation Order (ANO)

Details of legal regulations and requirements are published in the Air Navigation Order (ANO). The ANO is an Order of Parliament, amended as required.

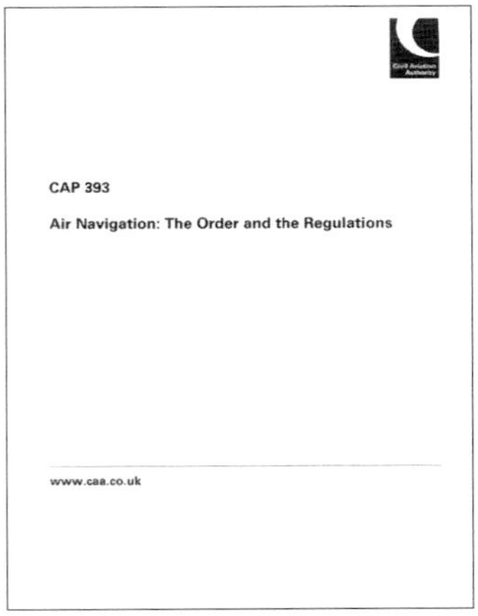

The Air Navigation Order is available as a CAA publication

▶ Revision

1 The detail of specific aviation laws is most likely to be found in which publication?

A Notices to Airmen (NOTAM)

B Aeronautical Information Circulars (AIC)

C The Air Navigation Order (ANO)

D Pre Flight Information Bulletins (PIB)

2 Information relevant to the daily flight operation of aircraft is disseminated to pilots and organisations by the:

A Aeronautical Information Service (AIS)

B Department of Transport (DfT)

C International Civil Aviation Organisation (ICAO)

D National Air Traffic Service (NATS)

3 The document which contains daily flight operation information for pilots is the:

A Air Navigation Order (ANO)

B Aeronautical Information Package (AIP)

C Rules of the Air

D Accident Investigation Regulations

4 Aeronautical Information Circulars are reissued after a certain period if they have not been replaced or revoked previously. The period is:

A 5 years

B 3 years

C 1 year

D 6 months

5 Which of the following subjects would you not expect to find in an Aeronautical Information Circular?

A A current Aeronautical Chart Catalogue

B Details of temporary restricted airspace

C Advice on the effect of some medication on pilot's ability

D Details of airfield facilities

6 Prior to flight a pilot is required to check that the route is suitable and there are no areas of temporarily active airspace which might have to be avoided. The best source of information to find out about the active airspace is:

A A NOTAM

B An AIC (GREEN)

C The Rules of the Air

D The ANO

Answers on page 169

Microlights

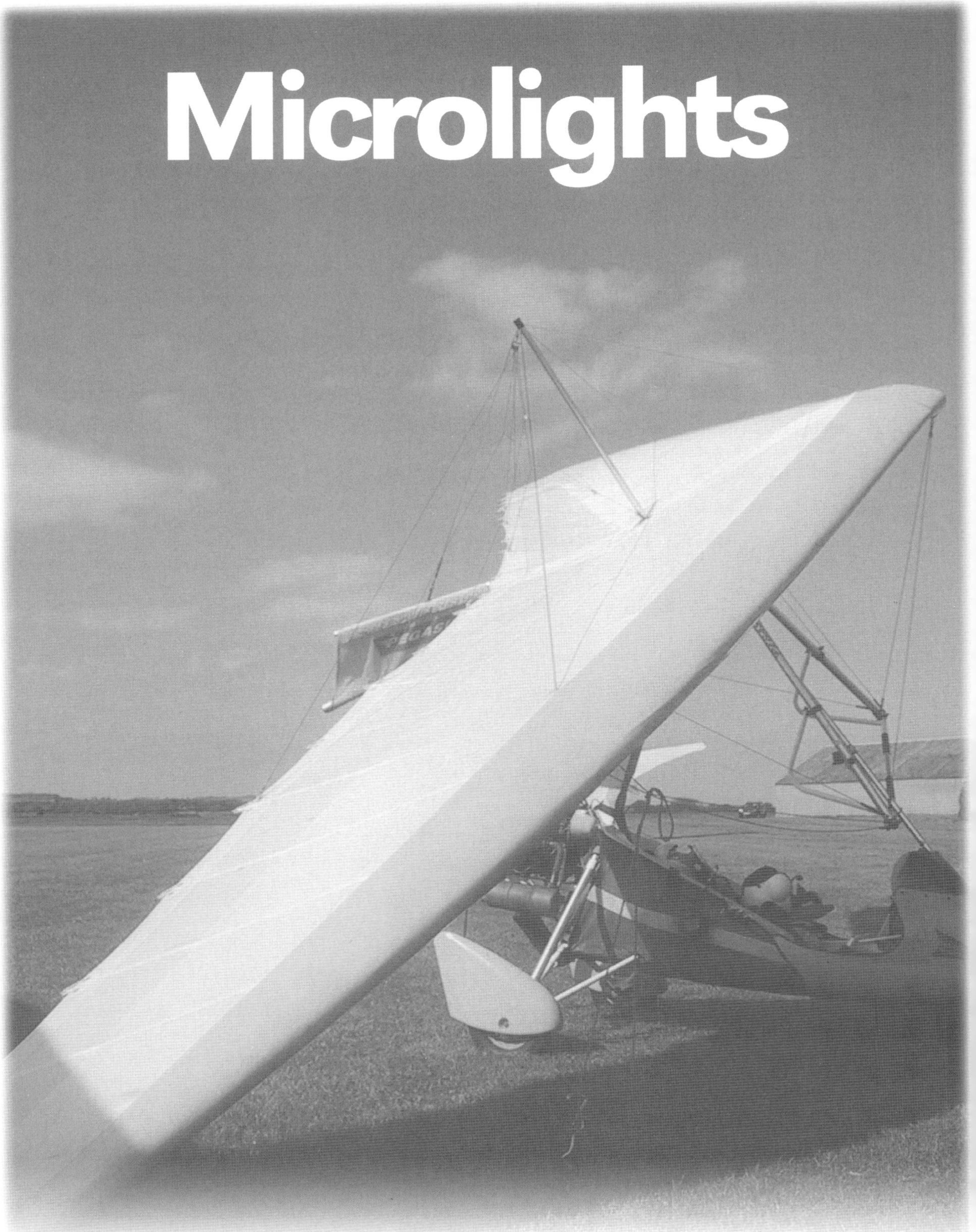

▶ Definition

▶ Definition

What is a microlight? A microlight is an aeroplane built within certain design parameters. Those parameters are:

- It may have one or two seats.
- A maximum total weight authorised (MTWA) of 450 kilograms for two seat aircraft and 300 kilograms for single seat where the aircraft is a landplane.
- A maximum total weight authorised (MTWA) of 495 kilograms for two seat aircraft and 330 kilograms for single seat where the aircraft is a floatplane or amphibian.
- A wing loading at maximum total weight authorised not exceeding 25 kilograms per square metre or a stalling speed at maximum total weight authorised not exceeding 35 knots Calibrated Air Speed (CAS). Wing loading is defined as the ratio of aircraft weight to wing area.

There are many different designs of aircraft all meeting the microlight definition.

Some different types of microlight

A powered parachute

© Keith Negal

The licence required to fly a microlight aircraft is, in the main, common to all types. There is of course an exception (isn't there always?) and that is for a sub-category of microlights called Powered Parachutes. Powered Parachutes are aircraft which use a ram air para-wing above a frame with a tricycle undercarriage, pilot seat and engine.

There is a further group of powered aircraft previously known as Foot Launched Powered Flying Machines (FLPFM) now known as Self Propelled Hang Gliders (SPHG). Although they meet the microlight definition, it is not necessary for the pilot to hold a licence to fly them in the UK. These aircraft are now classified as gliders and are subject to the same rules as applied to gliders operating within UK airspace.

A Foot Launched Powered Flying Machine, now known as a Self Propelled Hang Glider

Licences, Ratings and Authorities

XII	Ratings to be revalidated
Class	**Remarks/Restrictions**
Microlight Aeroplanes (Landplanes)	Nil
No further entries	No further entries

Licence: UK/NP/436964E/A Page 4 of 4 28/06/2006

Licences, Ratings and Authorities

- Licences
- Ratings
- Authorities

▶ Licences

A licence is granted by a regulating body and allows the holder of the licence to do whatever the licence has been issued to permit. A fishing licence lets you fish, a driving licence lets you drive and a pilot's licence lets you fly.

▶ Ratings

A rating is a qualification on a licence stipulating the detail of the intention of the licence. A pilot's licence has ratings entitling the holder of the licence to fly particular types of aircraft and may extend the privileges further, as in the case of an instructor rating. For example the National Private Pilot's Licence (NPPL) can be issued with any one of three aircraft ratings. These are:

- the Microlight rating;
- the Self Launched Motor Glider rating (SLMG) and;
- the Simple Single Engine Aircraft rating (SSEA).

A pilot may hold more than one rating on his or her licence.

▶ Authorities

An authority is granted to the holder by the authorising body as an appointment on their behalf. An example of an authority is an Examiner authority.

Pilot Licencing

Pilot Licencing

▶The National Private Pilot Licence

To fly a microlight in the UK you will need a Private Pilot Licence issued by the Civil Aviation Authority (CAA) with a valid rating covering Microlight Aircraft. The current licence is called the National Private Pilot Licence (NPPL) to which a microlight aircraft rating can be added. The NPPL can also be issued with a rating to fly simple single engine aircraft (SSEA) weighing up to 2000kg, and which are not microlights. A further rating is available to fly self launching motorised gliders (SLMG).

A NPPL licence holder may have more than one rating if he or she wishes to fly a variety of aircraft.

An NPPL

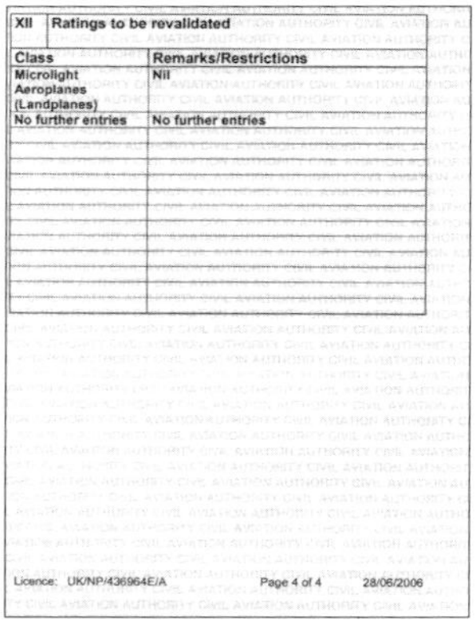

XII	Ratings to be revalidated
Class	Remarks/Restrictions
Microlight Aeroplanes (Landplanes)	Nil
No further entries	No further entries

Licence: UK/NP/436964E/A Page 4 of 4 28/06/2006

A rating entitling the holder to fly microlight landplanes

It is possible that in the future other aircraft groups may be added to the NPPL, for example Gyroplanes.

A pilot wishing to fly a Powered Parachute may do so on a Microlight aircraft rating or a Powered Parachute rating. A pilot with only a Power Parachute rating is not entitled to fly other types of microlight.

A pilot wishing to fly a Seaplane (capable of taking-off from, or landing on, water only) must complete differences training and have attained a pass in the Private or Professional Seamanship examination.

A pilot wishing to fly an Amphibian (capable of taking-off from, or landing on, both land or water,) must complete differences training and have attained pass in the Private or Professional Seamanship examination, however if the pilot only wishes to fly from a land aerodrome a differences training is not required.

The NPPL (Microlight) is valid for flight within the UK only. If you want to fly a microlight in other countries you must establish what licence is required in that country before you fly there. Most countries will accept the UK NPPL(M) to fly microlights in their airspace.

The NPPL is a lifetime licence although to exercise the privileges of the licence (in other words to use it), you must hold a valid medical certificate and maintain currency on type by flying at least the specified minimum time over a specified period or pass a flight test to prove your ability. Whichever you do will be recorded in your logbook or licence by an examiner. More details are given later in this chapter.

It is possible to use other UK-issued licences to fly microlights. The holder of a UK CAA PPL (Aeroplanes) or UK JAA PPL (Aeroplanes) with a valid rating for Single Engine Piston (SEP) aircraft may use the privileges of that licence to fly microlights also although microlight experience cannot be used to maintain the SEP rating.

▶Training for the NPPL(M)

The NPPL(M) is issued following the successful completion of a training course conducted by an instructor.

Student pilots may start logging instructional flights towards the grant of a licence at the age of fourteen, although they may not fly solo until the age of sixteen and may not hold a licence until they are seventeen.

Before flying solo under training the student pilot must hold a valid Medical Declaration of Health or Medical Certificate and must act in accordance with any requirements or limitations imposed by the Declaration or Certificate.

▶NPPL Microlight Training Syllabus

The detailed content of the course is set out in the NPPL Microlight Training Syllabus published by the British Microlight Aircraft Association (BMAA).

In summary, the main requirements are:

1. Flight training must be conducted by a flying instructor to a minimum of 25 hours total time. Total time required includes:
   - 10 hours solo flight
   - 5 hours navigation training
   - 3 hours solo navigation training to include two cross country flights of at least 40 nautical miles with an away landing at least 15 nautical miles from the aerodrome of departure. The flights are known as Qualifying Cross Country flights. The Qualifying Cross Country flights must be flown over different routes to different destinations.
2. Pass a General Skills Test (GST) with an authorised examiner. The GST flight time may be included in the total requirement of 25 hours although it cannot count towards the required 10 hours of solo flight time.

There is no minimum required time for dual flight training – in fact there is actually a solo-flight-only training program for use on aircraft where there is no dual seat equivalent. This is hardly used now, although in the early days of microlight flying, when there were no two seat aircraft, everyone learnt by the solo method.

The minimum required solo and navigation training must be carried out within nine months of the licence application being received by the CAA. If your course is extended, by poor weather for example, you may have to fly additional hours to enable you to log the minimum hours within the required period prior to the licence application date.

In addition to the flight training required there are five examinations in ground subjects. The subjects are Navigation, Meteorology, Aviation Law, Aeroplanes General and Human Performance and Limitations.

The examinations for the ground subject syllabus are multiple choice papers with a validity period of one year.

There is one other examination, an oral exam called 'Aeroplanes Part 2'. This is usually carried out by the flight examiner at the same time as the GST. The GST and oral exam must be completed within the 9 months prior to applying for your licence.

▶The NPPL(M) with Operational Limitations

There is another course for a licence with 'Operational Limitations'. The course has a minimum total flight training time of 15 hours with a minimum solo time of 7 hours. The course does not include any navigation flight training, although all the examinations are the same and the flight test is conducted to the same standard. The Operational Limitations are:

1. No passenger may be carried by the pilot.
2. No flight shall commence or continue unless;
   - The surface wind speed must be less than 15 knots
   - There must be no cloud below 1000ft above ground level over the take-off site, planned route or landing site
   - The flight must be conducted in a flight visibility of not less than 10 kilometres
3. The aeroplane shall not fly more than 8 nautical miles from the take-off site.

The passenger carrying limitation may be lifted when the pilot has completed at least 25 hours of total flight time including at least 10 hours solo. The pilot's logbook is then endorsed by a microlight flight examiner. There is no need to return the licence to the CAA.

The remaining operational limitations can be removed by completing the navigation training required in the full syllabus and the total times for required for that syllabus. The limitations are then removed from the licence by the CAA.

▶Training for the NPPL M (Powered Parachutes)

All training for a licence which includes a Powered Parachute rating must be carried out under the supervision of a Flying Instructor or Assistant Flying Instructor who holds a Powered Parachute instructor rating or microlight instructor rating.

The applicant must complete a syllabus of training recognised by the Civil Aviation Authority and pass a flight test and ground examinations.

Requirements for the NPPL(M) Powered Parachutes:

1. Flight training must be conducted by a flying instructor to a minimum of 15 hours total time. Total time required must include:
   - 6 hours solo flight
   - not less than 25 take-offs and full stop landings of which at least 6 must be as solo pilot in command (PIC).
   - 5 hours navigation training
   - 3 hours solo navigation training to include two cross country flights of at least 25 nautical miles with an away landing at least 10 nautical miles from the aerodrome of departure. The flights are known as Qualifying Cross Country flights. Qualifying Cross Country flights must be flown over different routes to different destinations.
2. Pass a General Skills Test (GST) with an authorised examiner. The GST flight time may be included in the total requirement of 15 hours although it cannot count towards the required 6 hours of solo flight time.

There is no minimum required time for dual flight training and there is a solo-flight-only training program for use on aircraft where there is no dual seat equivalent.

The minimum required solo and navigation training must be flown within nine months of the licence application being received by the CAA. If your course is extended, by poor weather for example, you may have to fly additional hours to enable you to have the minimum hours within the required period prior to the licence application date.

In addition to the flight training required there are examinations in five ground subjects. The subjects are Navigation, Meteorology, Aviation Law, Aeroplanes General and Human Performance and Limitations.

The examinations for the ground syllabus are multiple choice papers with a validity period of one year.

There is one other examination, an oral exam called Aeroplanes Part 2. This is carried out usually by the flight examiner at the same time as the GST. The GST and oral exam must be completed within 9 months prior to applying for your licence.

▶NPPL(M) Powered Parachutes with Operational Limitations

There is another course for a licence with Operational Limitations. That course has a minimum total flight training time required of 4 hours with a minimum solo time of 1 hour. The applicant must have completed at least 25 take-offs and landings, of which at least 6 must be as pilot in command (PIC). The course does not include any navigation flight training although all the examinations are the same and the flight test is conducted to the same standard. The operational limitations are:

1. No passenger may be carried by the pilot.
2. No flight shall commence or continue unless;
   - the surface wind speed is 10 knots or less,
   - there is no cloud below 1000 feet above ground level over the take off site, planned route or landing site,
   - the flight can be conducted in a flight visibility of not less than 10 kilometres.
3. The aeroplane shall not fly more than 8 nautical miles from the take-off site.

The passenger carrying limitation may be lifted when the pilot has completed at least 15 hours of total flight time including at least 6 hours solo. The pilot's logbook is endorsed by a microlight flight examiner to confirm that the required minimum has been achieved. There is no need to return the licence to the CAA.

The remaining operational limitations can be removed by completing the navigation training required in the full syllabus and the flight times for that syllabus. The limitations are then removed from the licence by the CAA.

▶Use of Aerodromes for Flying Instruction and Testing

Microlights are exempt from the requirement to use only licensed, government or CAA-owned or managed aerodromes for conducting instruction or testing for the grant of a licence or rating. The requirement to use a licenced (or government or CAA) aerodrome does apply to training for JAA licences and NPPL SSEA ratings. The exemption is published in an AIC, currently 70/2003 (White 85) issued in 2003.

▶Privileges of the Microlight Licence

The microlight licence allows the holder to act as Pilot in Command of microlight aircraft, as detailed in the ratings held, with the following limitations:

1. Flight must always be in accordance with the Visual Flight Rules (VFR) only;
2. Flight must be carried out in no less than 3 kilometres visibility at any time;
3. Flight must always be within sight of the surface;
4. No night flight permitted. 'Night' is defined the time from half an hour after sunset until half an hour before sunrise. Sunset and sunrise being determined at surface level;
5. Flight on a Special Visual Flight Rule (SVFR) clearance is only permitted with a minimum visibility not less than 10 kilometres;
6. No flight carrying passengers is permitted, unless within the preceding 90 days the holder has completed at least 3 take-offs and landings as sole manipulator of the controls in an aircraft of the same type;
7. A pilot who only has experience in aircraft with 'three axis' controls may not fly an aircraft with 'flex wing' controls until they have completed differences training and had that training recorded in their personal flying logbook;
8. A pilot who only has experience in aircraft with 'flex wing' controls may not fly an aircraft with 'three axis' controls until they have completed differences training and had that training recorded in their personal flying logbook;
9. No flight for reward is permitted unless the flight is an instructional or examination flight and the pilot holds the required instructor or examiner rating. Both the pilot and the student/candidate must be members of a flying club;
10. The pilot must have a valid medical certificate or declaration of health;
11. The pilot must have a valid Certificate of Test or Certificate of Experience.
12. A pilot wishing to fly from water must complete differences training and pass the Private or Professional Seamanship examination.

Specific detail of the Privileges and Conditions of the NPPL may be found in the Air Navigation Order, Schedule 8.

▶ Maintaining Licence Privileges

To allow the holder of a Private Pilot Licence with a Microlight Rating to maintain the privileges of that licence, the holder must hold a valid medical certificate or declaration of health and a valid Certificate of Test or Experience. These requirements also apply to the holders of other NPPL ratings and holders of a licence with a balloon or gyroplane rating.

▶ Medical Certificate

To maintain licence privileges the holder of a licence or a student pilot flying solo must have a valid medical certificate. The certificate may be a Class 1 or Class 2 issued by an Authorised Medical Examiner, (AME). An alternative to the medical certificate is a 'National Private Pilot Licence Declaration Of Medical Fitness To Fly' which is signed by the pilot and the pilot's General Practitioner (GP).

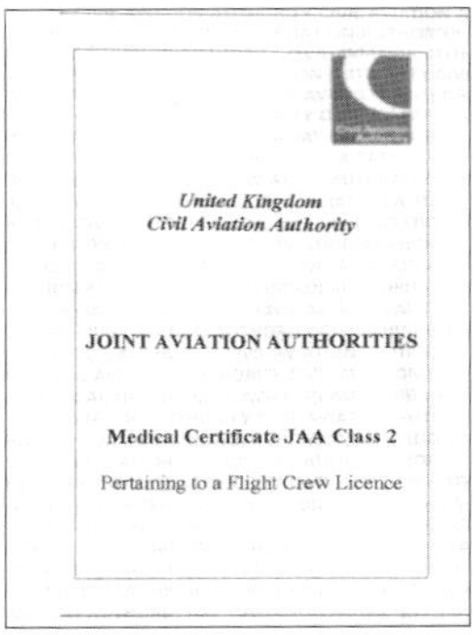
United Kingdom
Civil Aviation Authority

JOINT AVIATION AUTHORITIES

Medical Certificate JAA Class 2

Pertaining to a Flight Crew Licence

A Class 2 Medical Certificate

The Class 1 and 2 certificates are issued to an international standard by the CAA and are recognised as valid for flights in countries other than just the country of issue. The NPPL Medical Declaration is not an internationally recognised medical standard and is therefore only valid for the country of issue, the UK.

UNITED KINGDOM NATIONAL PRIVATE PILOT LICENCES
National PPL, PPL (Balloon & Airship), PPL (Gyroplane)
MEDICAL DECLARATION

PILOT SECTION:

Full Name

Date of birth (day/month/year) / /

I understand the "Notes for the Pilot" printed with this declaration. I have discussed my medical history with my GP and have not withheld any relevant medical information from him/her. I believe that I am fit to fly as a pilot at the standard indicated by my GP below.

Signature of pilot Date

GENERAL PRACTITIONER SECTION:

I am the general practitioner of the applicant named above and have seen his/her medical records. I have read "Notes for the General Practitioner" printed with this declaration and have had access to any appropriate information sheets.

I am aware of the DVLA medical requirements for professional and private drivers and believe that there is nothing in the applicant's medical history which prevents him/her meeting the following standard:

GP please tick one box only (the form is invalid if no, or both, boxes are ticked)

☐ Group 2 (professional driving). This standard allows solo flight and flight with passengers.

☐ Group 1 (private driving modified, if necessary, from an information sheet). This standard allows solo flight or flight with another qualified pilot as the only passenger.

Signature of doctor Date

Please print name

Practice stamp

Next medical assessment due on or before (please see notes)

Any special limitations (eg Aircraft modifications required due to physical disability)

A Medical Declaration

The standard of health required for the issue of a NPPL Medical Declaration is based on the requirements for vehicle drivers as published by the Driver and Vehicle Licensing Agency (DVLA). There are two standards against which a pilot may obtain a Medical Declaration: Professional Driver, classed as a Group 2 medical and Private Driver classed as Group 1 medical.

If the holder of the Declaration is judged as fit to fly solo or with passengers his declaration will be endorsed as Group 2.

If the holder is judged to be less fit his medical declaration will be endorsed as Group 1. A Group 1 pilot may only fly solo or with a qualified pilot who is the only passenger and who is able to take control of the aircraft from their seating position.

The period of validity of a Class 1 or 2 medical certificate is:

Age	Period of validity
Under 40	5 years
40 to 49	2 years
Age 50 to 69	12 months
Age 70 years and over	6 months

A five year certificate issued before the holder's 40th birthday is only valid until the holder's 42nd birthday.

The renewal period of a 'National Private Pilot's Licence Declaration of Medical Fitness to Fly' is:

Age	Renewal period
Up to, and including, age 44	Until 45th birthday or 5 years (whichever is the longer)
45 – 59	5 years
60 – 64	Until 65th birthday or 1 year (whichever is the longer)
65 and over	1 year

The holder must comply with any limitations imposed on the medical certificate.

The medical certificate is deemed to be suspended when:

- The holder suffers personal injury involving incapacity to undertake the functions as a member of the flight crew;
- The holder suffers illness involving incapacity to undertake those functions throughout a period of 21 days or more;
- The holder has reason to believe that she is pregnant.

The holder must inform the CAA in writing of such injury, illness or pregnancy, as soon as possible in the case of injury or pregnancy and as soon as a period of 21 days has elapsed in the case of illness.

The suspension shall cease, in the case of injury or illness, upon the holder being medically examined under arrangements made by the CAA and being pronounced fit to resume flight crew functions.

In the case of pregnancy the suspension may be lifted for periods specified by the CAA, subject to conditions. The suspension shall cease after the pregnancy and after the holder has been medically examined under arrangements made by the CAA and pronounced fit to resume flight crew functions.

▶ Certificate of Test

When a licence is issued it will have a page on which a record of the General Skills Test will be entered. The test validates the licence for a specified period from the date of the test.

▶ Certificate of Experience

A Certificate of Experience takes the form of an entry in the holder's licence to confirm that the holder had the required flight experience to maintain the privileges of the licence when the entry was made.

At the time of writing there is a proposed change to the minimum flight time requirements under discussion. I have included both the current and the proposed changed requirements here.

Current (2007):

The minimum flight time required is 5 hours within the 13 months following the date of the previous Certificate of Experience or Test. The 5 hours must include at least 3 hours as pilot in command (P1 or PIC), and may include up to 2 hours of flight with an instructor. Any hours flown with an instructor must be to a satisfactory standard and the instructor must sign the logbook to confirm that this is the case. The 5 hours must have been flown within the period of currency of the previous Certificate and within a period of no more than 13 months prior to the entry of the revalidating Certificate.

Proposed:

(It is not proposed to include gyroplanes in the changes)

The minimum flight time to maintain an aircraft rating by experience may become:

1. 12 hours in the 24 months following the date of the GST or the previous Certificate of Experience. The 12 hours must include at least:
   - 8 hours pilot in command
   - 1 hour of flight training with an instructor
   - 12 take-offs and landings
   - If the pilot does not complete the training element, but satisfies the other criteria, they will be restricted to flying aircraft fitted with a single seat only until such time as they complete the flight training.
2. The holder of more than one NPPL aircraft rating must fly at least one hour on each type for which a rating is held as part of the 12 hours minimum.

3. If the holder of the licence is unable to fly the required minimum time to maintain the licence validity they may fly a further flight test with an authorised examiner who will enter the details of the successful test on the licence page and so revalidate the licence for a further period. The flight test must be flown within the 3 months prior to the expiry of the rating to revalidate the rating for 24 months from the expiry date. A flight test flown more than 3 months prior to expiry, or after expiry, will revalidate the rating for 24 months from the date of the test.

Holders of more than one rating in the NPPL who cannot revalidate by experience must pass a flight test in each of the aircraft types for which they wish to revalidate the rating.

▶ Experience Requirement for PPL (Balloons)

The holder of a PPL (Balloons) must not fly as pilot in command of a free balloon unless, within the preceding 13 months, they have flown as pilot in command of a free balloon on at least 5 flights of at least 5 minutes duration each.

▶ Renewal by Certificate of Test

The holder of a licence who has been unable to revalidate the aircraft rating by experience or test within the validity period can renew the aircraft rating by test with an examiner. The content of the test varies slightly dependent on the period since which the holder last flew as pilot in command. At the time of writing the actual requirements are under review. Requirements will be published in the CAA publication, LASORS, to which you should refer.

A rating renewed by test will be valid for the same period as one revalidated by experience, with the period starting from the date of the test.

▶ Revision

7 Pilot licences have aircraft ratings included in them. To exercise the privileges of an aircraft rating the pilot must also hold:

A A current Radio Operators Licence and Medical Certificate

B A current Medical Certificate or Declaration of Health

C A current Radio operators Licence and a Declaration of Health

D A Medical Certificate or Declaration of Health and fully comprehensive insurance

8 A National Private Pilot's Licence is valid for:

A 3 years

B 5 years

C 10 years

D The lifetime of the holder

9 A Radio Operators Licence issued at the same time as a Private Pilot's Licence is valid for:

A 3 years

B 5 years

C 10 years

D The same validity period as the licence to a maximum of 10 years

10 An aircraft rating can be revalidated by:

A Passing a written examination

B Paying a revalidation fee online

C Flying a specified minimum flight time over a given period or flying a revalidation flight test with a flight examiner

D Flying a minimum flight time supervised by a flying instructor

11 The NPPL Microlight aircraft rating is valid for flight:

A Within the UK only

B Within Europe

C Within ICAO member states only

D Worldwide

12 A NPPL Medical Declaration is signed by the holder and one other person. That person must be:

A Any General Practitioner (GP)

B The holder's regular General Practitioner (GP)

C Any Professional person eg Solicitor, Priest etc

D A CAA Authorised Medical Examiner (AME)

13 An NPPL medical declaration with a Group 1 endorsement allows the holder to fly:

A Solo only

B Solo or with an instructor only

C Solo or with any passenger

D Solo or with a passenger who is also a qualified pilot and is able to control the aircraft from their seating position

---

14 An NPPL medical declaration issued to a pilot aged 23 is valid until the holder is aged:

A 28

B 33

C 45

D 60

---

15 An NPPL medical declaration issued to a pilot aged 46 is valid for how many years?

A 1

B 2

C 5

D 10

---

16 An NPPL medical declaration issued to a pilot aged 66 is valid for how many years?

A 1

B 2

C 5

D 10

---

17 If a person becomes ill or incapacitated for a specified period of time, or longer, the medical is deemed to be suspended. That period of illness is:

A 14 days

B 21 days

C 31 days

D 90 days

---

18 The holder of a NPPL may also use which other Medical Certificate instead of the Declaration of Health?

A Class 1 only

B Class 2 only

C Class 3 only

D Class 1 or 2

19 To obtain a NPPL with a Microlight Aircraft rating the student pilot must complete training to which syllabus?

A BMAA NPPL Microlight Syllabus

B JAR NPPL Syllabus

C AOPA NPPL Syllabus

D Any of the above

---

20 The Microlight training syllabus requires a minimum of how many hours solo flying for a licence without restrictions?

A 5

B 7

C 10

D 25

---

21 How many hours of cross country training must be completed for the initial issue of a NPPL with a Microlight rating without Operational Limitations, and how many of those must be solo?

A 3 and 1

B 5 and 3

C 6 and 3

D 5 and 0

---

22 An NPPL(M) may be issued with Operational Limitations. Which of the following are included in the restrictions?

A No passenger may be carried. No flight in less than 13 kilometres visibility

B No flight in less than 10 kilometres visibility. No flight when the surface wind is more than 15 knots

C No flight beyond 8 kilometres of take-off

D No flight when the cloud base is less than 1000 feet above ground level and the wind is greater than 5 knots

---

The NPPL with a Microlight rating allows the holder to fly microlight aircraft with certain conditions applied. Select which of the following are correct:

---

23 Minimum in flight visibility for the holder of an unrestricted microlight rating:

A 1.5 kilometres

B 3 kilometres

C 5 kilometres

D 10 kilometres

---

24 Minimum in-flight visibility when flying on a Special Visual Flight Rule clearance for the holder of an unrestricted microlight rating:

A 1.5 kilometres

B 3 kilometres

C 8 kilometres

D 10 kilometres

25 A pilot may not carry passengers unless within the preceding "X" days he or she has made at least "Z" take-offs and landings as sole manipulator of the controls of an aeroplane of the same type. X and Z represent which numbers?

A 30 & 3

B 60 & 6

C 90 & 3

D 90 & 6

---

26 The holder of an NPPL licence may fly the aircraft out of sight of the surface:

A When above cloud

B At night

C Under the control of an Air Traffic Control service

D Never

---

27 If the holder of the licence has been trained on, and only has experience of flying, aircraft with flexwing controls they:

A May fly an aircraft with 3 axis controls at their discretion with no requirement for formal training

B May only fly 3 axis controlled aircraft having completed differences training which must be recorded in their logbook

C May only fly 3 axis aircraft after completing a minimum of 25 hours of conversion with a flying instructor

D Must pass a General Skills Test (GST) conducted by a flight examiner and apply for an additional rating to be added to their licence

---

28 The holder of the NPPL may not fly the aircraft:

A At night

B In Visual Meteorological Conditions

C In controlled airspace

D In Class F airspace

---

29 The minimum age to fly solo as part of an NPPL(M) course is:

A 14

B 17

C 16

D 18

---

30 A pilot who holds an NPPL(M) with Operational Limitations may carry passengers:

A Never

B After flying 10 hours solo

C When authorised by a flying instructor

D Provided the aircraft remains within 8 nautical miles of the departure airfield

---

Answers on page 169

Licence Considerations

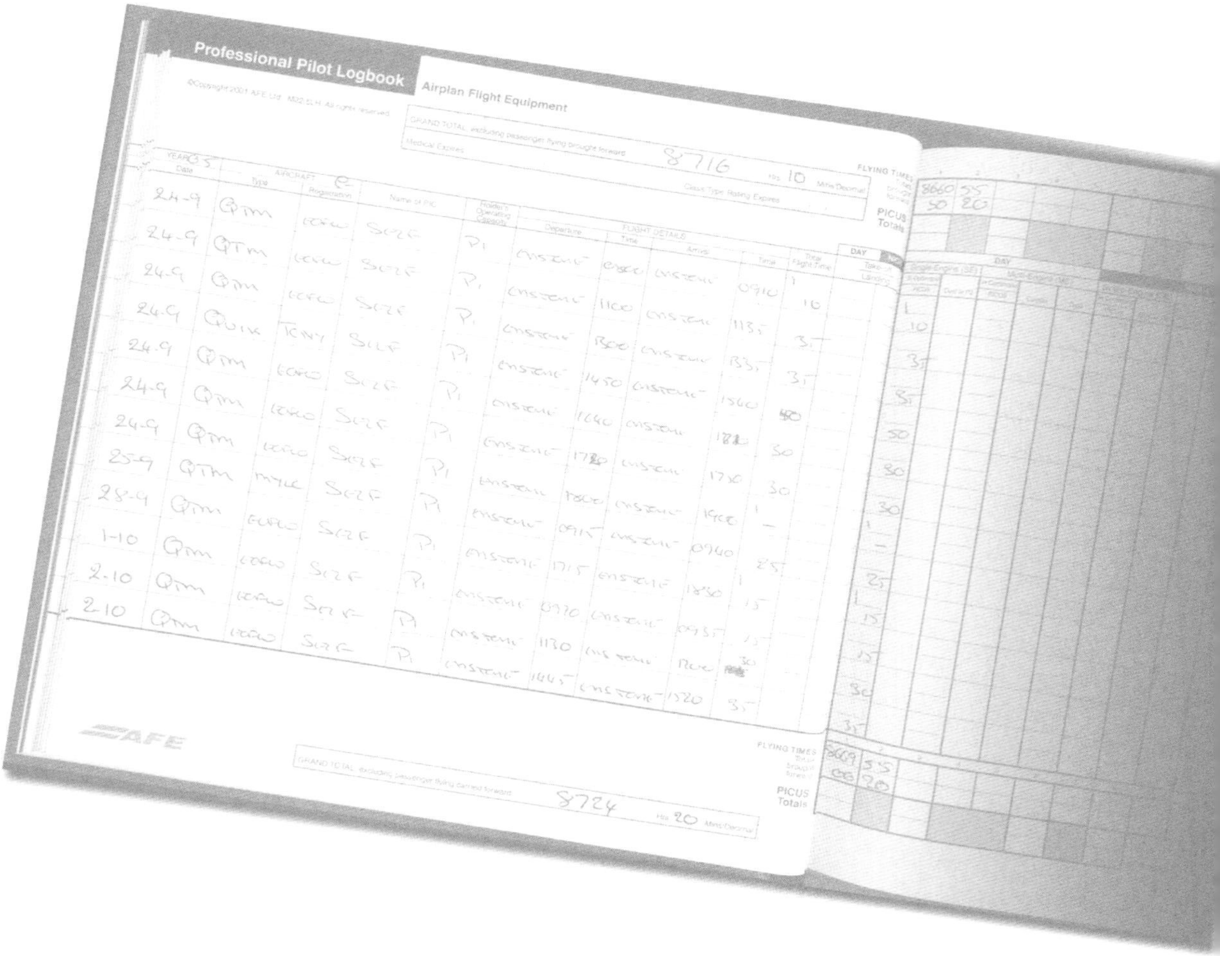

Licence Considerations

- Exhibitions of Flying
- Public Transport and Aerial Work
- Charity Flights
- Pilot Logbook
- Revision

▶ Exhibitions of Flying

An article of the ANO deals with civil flying displays within the United Kingdom. Where a flying display is at an advertised event open to the public, the article places responsibilities on both the organiser of the flying display and the participating pilots. The flying display director, the organiser, must obtain the permission in writing of the CAA and civil display pilots must hold a Display Authorisation (DA).

The Display Authorisation is available to pilots who successfully complete an evaluation by a Display Pilot evaluator appointed by the CAA.

Balloon events, whether a tethered display, air race or contest, do not require a permission under the Air Navigation Order.

▶ Public Transport and Aerial Work

A flight is deemed to be for the purpose of public transport or aerial work if money is given or promised for the flight. As a private pilot, you may not carry out a public transport or aerial work flight. However, you may accept a contribution towards the direct cost of the flight by a person sharing the flight with you. The contribution may be up to, but no more than, 50% of the direct cost of the flight payable by you.

▶ Charity Flights

A charity flight is a flight for which money is collected and donated to a registered charity. All money collected must be donated to the charity. A general permission has been granted to allow such flights to be treated as private flights even though payment has been made for the flight.

Details of the precise requirements and conditions for conducting charity flights may be found in an Aeronautical Information Circular (AIC), currently 11/2007 (White 132) issued in 2007.

UNITED KINGDOM

AERONAUTICAL INFORMATION CIRCULAR

AIC 79/2005
(White 114)
15 September

National Air Traffic Services Ltd
Aeronautical Information Service
Control Tower Building, London Heathrow Airport
Hounslow, Middlesex TW6 1JJ
Editorial: 020-8745 3457
Distribution: 0870-8871410 (Documedia Solutions Ltd)
Content: 01293-573540 (GAD)
Web site: www.ais.org.uk

Cancels AIC 76/2003 (White 66)

CHARITY FLIGHTS

1 Article 159 of the Air Navigation Order 2005 makes provision for certain fund raising flights on behalf of registered charities to be flown as private flights. They are therefore excluded from the commercial air transport regulations in respect of the carriage of passengers and from the aerial work regulations in respect of sponsored flights without passengers. They may be conducted in accordance with the conditions of a Permission issued by the CAA, by:

- the holder of a Private Pilot's Licence;
- professionally licensed pilots; or
- pilots of gliders and hang gliders holding certificates issued by their respective associations.

2 The types of flights which the provisions and the term 'Charity Flights' encompass are:

- the carriage of passengers, which includes children of all ages, on flights for which no payment is made to the operator or pilot of the aircraft but for which the passengers make a payment, all of which is contributed to a registered charity; or
- the carriage of passengers on a flight as a prize in a lottery, the total proceeds of which go to a registered charity; or
- a sponsored flight, either with or without passengers, for which the total proceeds go to a registered charity.

3 For the purposes of this Circular and the General Permission, the term 'registered charity' includes exempt and excepted charities, all as defined by the Charity Commission. Further information can be found on the www.charity-commission.gov.uk Web site.

4 While Article 159 clarifies the legislation and also represents a considerable relaxation of the commercial air transport and aerial work regulations, the CAA has a responsibility for maintaining standards of safety, particularly where the carriage of passengers is concerned.

5 Certain general conditions for various categories of aircraft, listed at the Annexes, have been set as criteria for a charity flight which should be regarded as normal guidelines. The Annexes also indicate those areas where applicants are required to submit their own proposals for consideration.

6 A General Permission attached to this Circular satisfies the Article 159 requirement for CAA permission in writing before conducting a charity flight provided that the criteria listed at the Annexes to this Circular are met. This Circular contains revised pilot experience and currency criteria to reflect JAR-FCL requirements.

7 The Annexes do NOT provide for the carriage of passengers on charity flights in:

- powered aircraft which do not hold a valid Certificate of Airworthiness (a Permit to Fly is not acceptable);
- powered aeroplanes from unlicensed aerodromes;
- a glider, the airworthiness of which has not been established to the satisfaction of the BGA;
- hang gliders, paragliders and microlights, including powered parachutes.

Specific requests will be considered by the CAA before a decision is made.

8 With regard to charity flights in special-shaped balloons, specific requests will be considered by the CAA before a decision is made.

9 Any person may carry out a charity flight, provided that the general conditions in respect of a particular category of aircraft can be met. For proposed flights which might not satisfy the conditions, the form at Annex 8 to this Circular, or photocopies of it, may be used as may typed or manuscript applications giving the same details.

9.1 Completed applications should be sent to: Civil Aviation Authority, General Aviation Department, Operations Section, Aviation House (1W), South Area, London Gatwick Airport, West Sussex, RH6 0YR (Tel: 01293-573526, Fax: 01293-573973).

10 Maximum possible advance notice should be given for applications (normally not less than 28 days).

11 The organiser is to ensure that the necessary permission (either under the General Permission or by application) is in place prior to any flight tickets being sold, bid for, auctioned or drawn.

12 Prospective passengers must be made aware that flights do not fully comply with commercial air transport regulations.

13 The material in this Circular (at Appendices 1 to 4 of Annex 3) gives additional guidance for helicopter pilots operating from sites other than established airfields. The diagrams and performance figures are closely allied to those currently used for commercial air transport pleasure flying operations but should always be used in conjunction with the relevant Flight Manual figures.

This Circular is issued for information, guidance and necessary action.

Printed and distributed by Documedia Solutions Ltd, Cheltenham, Glos.

1

AIC contain information on administrative and safety matters.

The AIC gives details of the requirements for some types of aircraft operation when engaged in charity flights:

Without passengers:

	Pilot	Aircraft	Aerodrome	Weather	Aircraft Limitations
	Valid Licence 100hrs PIC 10hrs on type	C of A or Permit	Any	VMC	As Permit
	BHPA Club Certificate or higher Current medical	Any	Any	BHPA minima	BHPA minima
	BGA Bronze C 50hrs PIC Current medical	Accepted by BGA	Any	BGA minima	BGA minima
	10hrs PIC	As C of A	Any	Any	VMC

With passengers:

	Pilot	Aircraft	Aerodrome	Weather	Aircraft Limitations
	BGA Silver C 100hrs PIC Current medical – NPPL Group 2 1 hour or 5 flights as PIC in last 30 days age under 70	Accepted by BGA	BGA recognised	BGA minima and not less than: 2000ft ceiling Max cable launch to 500ft below cloud Max 75% of surface and cross wind limits	VMC No aerobatics A to A only Within 5nm Max 3 flights per pilot per day
	Valid licence Under 60 years of age 20hrs PIC post licence 3 free flights PIC on class in last 90 days, not less than 5 minutes Current medical – NPPL Group 2	C of A in Transport or Private	No obstructions within 500m downwind Crowd free 30m	Minimum cloud ceiling 2000ft Minimum vis 3km Max surface wind 10kt	VMC only Max pilot plus 4 passengers Max 3 flights per day per pilot
			NOT ALLOWED		
			NOT ALLOWED		

▶ Pilot Logbook

It is a requirement that a pilot maintains a record of flights in a pilot logbook. The detail required to be entered in the logbook is:

- The date of the flight
- The type of aircraft flown
- The registration of the aircraft
- The name of the captain
- The capacity in which the pilot acted. If in charge that capacity is P1, if under training PUT, if completing a successful test with an examiner P1S (pilot under supervision)
- The place of departure and arrival
- Time of departure and arrival
- The time spent in flight
- Details of any training or examination undertaken on the flight

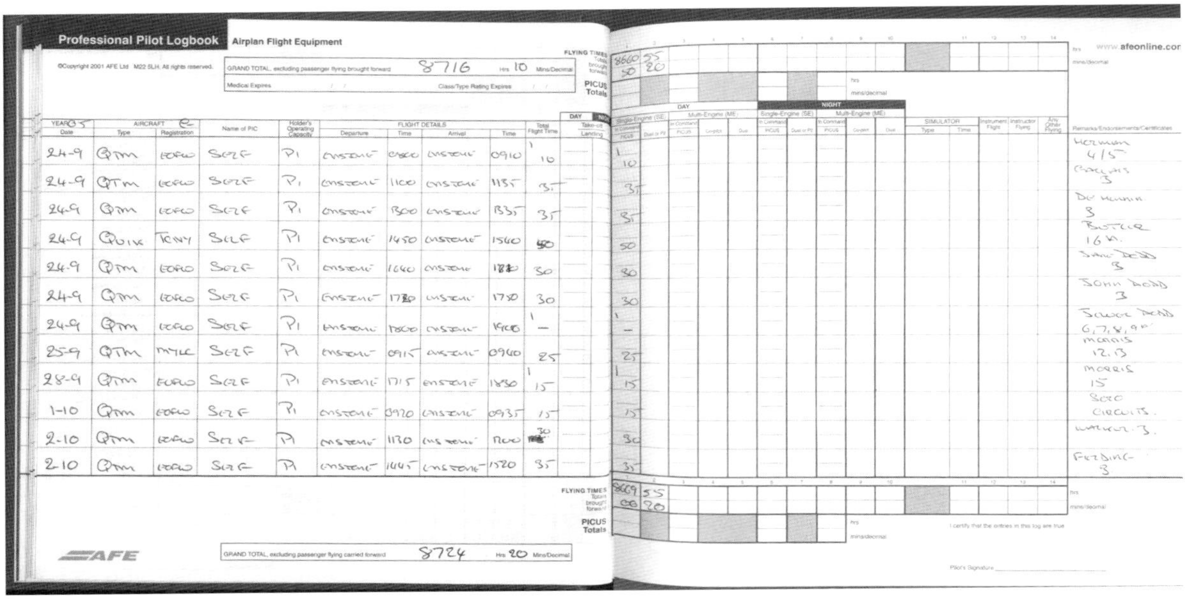

You may include in the logbook other details such as passenger name, route, etc if you wish. A logbook must be kept for at least two years after the last entry made in it.

It is an offence (as with other documents), to make a false entry, leave-out a required entry, alter an entry, deface an entry or destroy the logbook during the period for which it is required to be kept.

Logbooks may be inspected by authorised persons including members of the police.

▶ Revision

31 A display pilot authorisation is required by a pilot displaying an aircraft when:

A The event has attracted, or is likely to attract, more than 500 people

B The event is open and advertised to the public and more than 500 people are expected

C The event is open and advertised to the public and more than 1000 people are expected

D The event is open and advertised to the public however many people are expected

32 A charity flight is a flight which:

A Because money is raised in respect of the flight would normally be considered to be aerial work but is considered to be a private flight

B Donates some of the money raised to a good cause

C May allow the aircraft to fly in conditions and over areas not normally allowed because the flight is raising money for a good cause

D Can only be flown by an instructor

33 Charity flights in microlights require the pilot to have a certain minimum experience

A Hold a licence and have 50 hours of pilot in command

B Hold a licence and have 75 hours of pilot in command and at least 5 hours on type

C Hold a licence and have 100 hours of pilot in command and at least 5 hours on type

D Hold a licence and have 100 hours of pilot in command and at least 10 hours on type

34 It is a legal requirement for pilots of powered aircraft for which a licence is required to be held to maintain a personal flying logbook. The logbook is required to contain certain details of the flight. Which of the following best represent items to be recorded?

A Names of the pilot and passenger. Duration of flight. Place of take-off and landing.

B Place of take-off and landing. Time of take-off and landing. Name of authorising pilot. Details of navigation routings.

C Registration of the aircraft. Type of aircraft. Names of pilot and passenger.

D Registration and type of aircraft. Captain's name. Training exercises or tests carried out

35 The logbook must be retained by the pilot for a minimum period after the last entry made in it. That time is:

A 1 year

B 2 years

C 5 years

D 10 years

36 The logbook must be available to be inspected by:

A Any Flying Instructor

B Any Flying Examiner

C A policeman

D A magistrate

37 It is an offence to:

A Deliberately omit a flight entry

B Start a new logbook before the previous one is completely full

C Write in red pen in the logbook

D Write details of the flight not required by law to be entered in the book

Answers on page 169

Instructor Ratings (Microlights) and Examiner Authorities

Instructor Ratings (Microlights) and Examiner Authorities

- ▶ Flying Instructor Rating (FI)
- ▶ Assistant Flying Instructor Rating (AFI)
- ▶ Commercial Licence
- ▶ Flying Instructor Course Instructors
- ▶ Examiner Authorities
- ▶ Revision

▶ Flying Instructor Rating (FI)

The Flying Instructor Rating entitles the holder to give instruction in flying in microlight aircraft for the purpose of the student pilot gaining a NPPL(M).

The FI rating is not type restricted to weight shift or three axis controlled microlights although common sense says that the instructor should be able to fly the aircraft type to flight test standard before attempting to teach on it.

The FI rating is valid for 25 months and is revalidated by completing an instructor revalidation test with an FIE (Flying Instructor Examiner).

▶ Assistant Flying Instructor Rating (AFI)

An Assistant Flying Instructor Rating entitles the holder to give instruction in flying in microlight aircraft for the purpose of the student pilot gaining a NPPL with a microlight rating. The AFI may conduct all the flight training exercises included in the NPPL Microlights syllabus including navigation training to other aerodromes. However, the AFI has limitations to his/her rating privileges. These are:

- The AFI may only instruct under the direct supervision of a Flying Instructor (FI) who is present at the airfield at which the instruction takes place during the take-off and landing of the instructional flight. The supervising instructor is expected to be able to fly the type of aircraft used by the AFI and should have at least 5 hours teaching experience on that type.
- The AFI may not authorise or give any flight direction to a student pilot for their first solo flight or their first solo cross country flight. For this purpose a cross country flight is any flight that goes more than 3 miles from the airfield, although not all flights of more than 3 miles from the airfield may be considered to count towards the cross country training requirements. Only flights that have been properly pre-planned can be counted towards the cross country requirements.
- An AFI may not supervise another AFI.

An AFI rating is obtained by the pilot completing a course of training with a Flying Instructor Course (FIC) approved flight instructor and then passing an examination conducted by a Flying Instructor Examiner (FIE).

The AFI rating will initially restrict the AFI to teaching on the type of microlight that the course was conducted on which will be either weight shift or three axis controlled. The AFI may have the other type added to the rating by completing another test on that additional type. The additional type test may be conducted by an FIC instructor who does not have to be an FIE.

The AFI rating is valid for 13 months and is renewed by completing an instructor test with an FIE.

An AFI may upgrade to a FI by completing at least 100 hours of supervised flight instruction over a period of no less than 10 months and then passing an instructor test with an FIE.

A pilot must have held a licence for at least 8 months prior to starting the AFI course. The licence must not have Operational Limitations at the start of the course. The pilot must have 100 hours P1 prior to starting the course including at least 60 hours P1 in microlights.

▶ Commercial Licence

Microlight instructors are not required to hold a commercial licence in order to charge for their services as a pilot whilst conducting lessons or tests because their licences include the privilege to be remunerated for such flights.

There is no commercial licence currently available for microlight pilots, so other than for instruction or testing no person may be remunerated for services as a microlight pilot.

▶ Flying Instructor Course Instructors

A Flying Instructor Course instructor rating (FIC) entitles the holder to conduct training towards the grant of an Assistant Flying Instructor rating.

The Assistant Flying Instructor Course (AFIC) must be conducted at an approved Flight Training Organisation (FTO) which will be inspected annually by the CAA to confirm that it meets the required standards.

▶ Examiner Authorities

There are four examiner authorities which may be issued by the CAA.

R Examiner Authority (R)	Allows the holder to sign Certificates of Experience to confirm a pilot's flight hours to maintain the privileges of their licence.
GR Examiner Authority (GR)	Allows the holder to sign Certificates of Experience to confirm a pilot's flight hours to maintain the privileges of their licence and to conduct the ground examinations for the grant of a NPPL or PPL.
FE Examiner Authority	Allows the holder to sign Certificates of Experience to confirm a pilot's flight hours to maintain the privileges of their licence and to conduct the ground examinations for the grant of a NPPL or PPL. The FE may also conduct flight tests for the grant or renewal of a NPPL or PPL as appropriate.
Flying Instructor Examiner Authority (FIE)	Allows the holder to conduct flight tests for the grant or revalidation of an Instructor Rating.

The period of validity of Examiner Authorities is currently 3 years (as at 2007).

▶ Revision

38 The minimum requirements for entry to an Assistant Flying Instructor Course are:

A Hold a NPPL(M) and have at least 50 hours Pilot in Command experience

B Hold a licence valid for microlights and have at least 75 hours Pilot in Command experience

C Hold a licence valid for microlights and have at least 100 hours Pilot in Command experience

D Hold a licence valid for microlights and have at least 150 hours Pilot in Command experience

39 The holder of an Assistant Flying Instructor Rating may:

A Authorise student's first solo and subsequent solo flights

B Conduct cross country training

C Operate without direct supervision of the holder of a Flying Instructor rating

D Supervise another instructor

40 To revalidate a Flying Instructor rating the holder must complete a test with a Flying Instructor Examiner (FIE). The Assistant Flying Instructor Rating is valid for "X" months, the Flying Instructor Rating is valid for "Z" months. The value of "X" and "Z" are:

A 10 & 20

B 13 & 13

C 25 & 25

D 13 & 25

41 Microlight pilots are required to have their aircraft ratings revalidated periodically. Revalidation may be by flight experience which is then confirmed by an examiner signing the rating page included in the licence. Which microlight examiners can sign the rating page?

A R only

B R and GR only

C Flight Examiners only

D R, GR and Flight Examiners

Answers on page 169

Aircraft Registration and Airworthiness

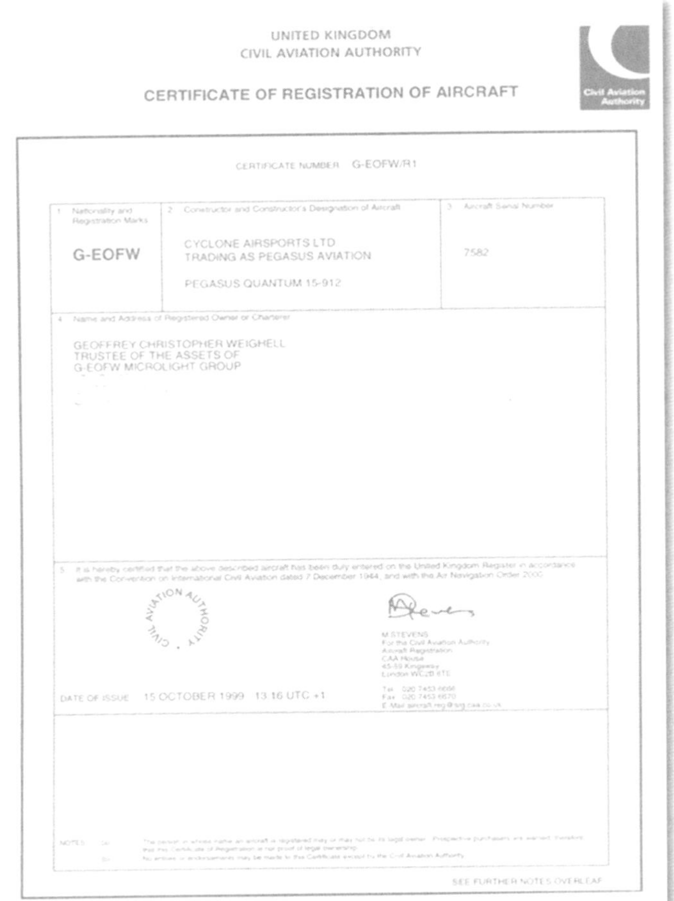

UNITED KINGDOM
CIVIL AVIATION AUTHORITY

CERTIFICATE OF REGISTRATION OF AIRCRAFT

Civil Aviation Authority

CERTIFICATE NUMBER G-EOFW/R1

1 Nationality and Registration Marks	2 Constructor and Constructor's Designation of Aircraft	3 Aircraft Serial Number
G-EOFW	CYCLONE AIRSPORTS LTD TRADING AS PEGASUS AVIATION PEGASUS QUANTUM 15-912	7582

4 Name and Address of Registered Owner or Charterer

GEOFFREY CHRISTOPHER WEIGHELL
TRUSTEE OF THE ASSETS OF
G-EOFW MICROLIGHT GROUP

5 It is hereby certified that the above described aircraft has been duly entered on the United Kingdom Register in accordance with the Convention on International Civil Aviation dated 7 December 1944, and with the Air Navigation Order 2000

CIVIL AVIATION AUTHORITY

M STEVENS
For the Civil Aviation Authority
Aircraft Registration
CAA House
45-59 Kingsway
London WC2B 6TE

Tel: 020 7453 6666
Fax: 020 7453 6670
E-Mail aircraft.reg@srg.caa.co.uk

DATE OF ISSUE 15 OCTOBER 1999 13.16 UTC +1

NOTES (a) The person in whose name an aircraft is registered may or may not be its legal owner. Prospective purchasers are warned, therefore, that this Certificate of Registration is not proof of legal ownership.

(b) No entries or endorsements may be made to this Certificate except by the Civil Aviation Authority.

SEE FURTHER NOTES OVERLEAF

Aircraft Registration and Airworthiness

▶ Registration of Aircraft

Registration on microlight aircraft

All microlights, gyroplanes and balloons flying in the UK must be registered. To register an aircraft in the UK, an application form is completed with the details of the aircraft and owner (s) and forwarded to the UK CAA Aircraft Registration department. The aircraft is entered onto the register and allotted a registration consisting of the letters G (to represent the UK), followed by four other letters. It is possible, by paying a little extra, to have an out of sequence, personalised sequence, such as G-EOFW. A registration document is issued to the owner of the aircraft.

Maintaining the details of the owner(s) and aircraft is the responsibility of the owner (s) and not the CAA. If an owner changes address or sells the aircraft as a whole or a share, the CAA must be notified and the registration records and document will be amended as required.

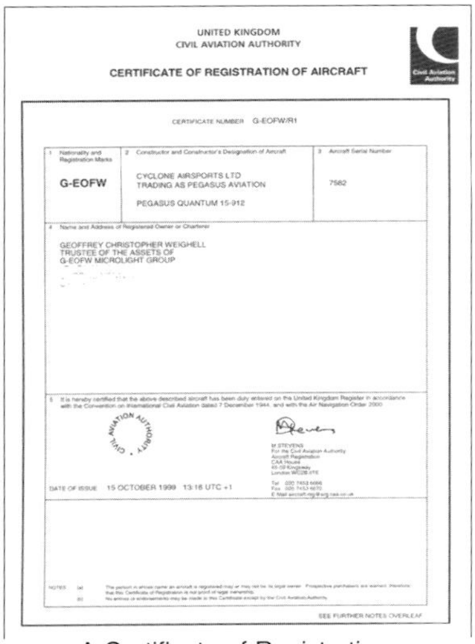

UNITED KINGDOM
CIVIL AVIATION AUTHORITY

CERTIFICATE OF REGISTRATION OF AIRCRAFT

CERTIFICATE NUMBER G-EOFW/R1

1 Nationality and Registration Marks	2 Constructor and Constructor's Designation of Aircraft	3 Aircraft Serial Number
G-EOFW	CYCLONE AIRSPORTS LTD TRADING AS PEGASUS AVIATION PEGASUS QUANTUM 15-912	7562

4 Name and Address of Registered Owner or Charterer

GEOFFREY CHRISTOPHER WEIGHELL
TRUSTEE OF THE ASSETS OF
G-EOFW MICROLIGHT GROUP

5 It is hereby certified that the above described aircraft has been duly entered on the United Kingdom Register in accordance with the Convention on International Civil Aviation dated 7 December 1944, and with the Air Navigation Order 2000

CIVIL AVIATION AUTHORITY

M STEVENS
For the Civil Aviation Authority
Aircraft Registration
CAA House

DATE OF ISSUE 15 OCTOBER 1999 13:18 UTC +1

SEE FURTHER NOTES OVERLEAF

A Certificate of Registration

Many microlights are owned by just one person, however with the increasing cost of the current high performance aircraft there is an increase in the number of aircraft which are owned by more than one individual. There are a couple of points to bear in mind when forming a group to own an aircraft.

Firstly, the law requires that the minimum share that an owner may have is 5% of the aircraft value. This limits the number of persons who may own a share in a particular aircraft to 20. This rule prevents unscrupulous operators avoiding airworthiness requirements in certain commercial instances.

Secondly, there are two ways in which the aircraft may be registered. It may be registered to all the individuals in the group. Each owner will then be listed on the Registration Certificate. If there is a change in ownership, a person leaving or joining the group for example, the aircraft must be re-registered to the new make-up of individuals. This will incur a CAA registration fee. The alternative is to register the aircraft to a named group such as "Enstone Microlight Group" and nominate one owner as the trustee of the group. The registration document will refer to the group as the owner with only the name of the trustee actually on the document. If there are any changes to the make up of the group the trustee will notify the CAA who will revise their records but not issue a new registration certificate. There is no fee for this change to the details.

The registration marks must be displayed on the aircraft, they must not be obscured and must be clear to read. Precise details of regulations regarding registration marks are detailed in the ANO.

▶ Airworthiness of Aircraft

To ensure that microlight aircraft are built and maintained to a safe standard, they are required to comply with stipulated airworthiness standards. For microlights the details are currently found in a document called British Civil Airworthiness Requirements (BCAR) Section S. Aircraft which are shown to comply with these requirements may be issued with an airworthiness document called a 'Permit To Fly'.

Certificate No. PR 051324/002

UNITED KINGDOM
CIVIL AVIATION AUTHORITY

PERMIT TO FLY AND NOISE CERTIFICATE

Nationality and Registration Marks	Constructor and Constructor's Designation of Aircraft	Aircraft Serial Number
G-EOFW	CYCLONE AIRSPORTS LTD TRADING AS PEGASUS AVIATION PEGASUS QUANTUM 15-912	7582

This Permit to Fly is issued subject to the associated Conditions.

EXEMPTION

A CERTIFICATE OF VALIDITY FORMS PART OF THIS PERMIT TO FLY

NOISE CERTIFICATE

Date: 11 OCTOBER 2004

for the Civil Aviation Authority

A Permit to Fly

The Permit to Fly is issued to a new aircraft following an initial inspection and flight test. This is usually carried out by the factory producing the aircraft, or if it is a home built microlight, by the appointed inspector for the project. Attached to the Permit to Fly will be a document called a 'Certificate of Validity' which has a validity of one year. The Permit is only valid when it has an in-date, current, Certificate of Validity.

UNITED KINGDOM
CIVIL AVIATION AUTHORITY

CERTIFICATE OF VALIDITY – PERMIT TO FLY

Nationality and Registration Marks	Aeroplane Serial No.
G-EOFW	7582
Constructor and Constructor's Designation of Aeroplane: Cyclone Airsports LTD T/A Pegasus Aviation Pegasus Quantum 15-912	

~~*The microlight has been newly constructed and the Permit to Fly validated for the period shown below.~~

*It is hereby confirmed that the above mentioned aeroplane has been examined by the British Microlight Aircraft Association and was found, at the time of its inspection and flight testing, to be in a satisfactory and airworthy condition, and the Permit to Fly validated for the period shown below.

This Certificate forms part of the Civil Aviation Authority Permit to Fly No. PR 051324-002 and is effective

From 15/10/05 To 14/10/06

*Delete as applicable

Signed T. Hadebelden Dated 7/10/05

(For and on behalf of the British Microlight Aircraft Association)

CAA Approval Reference No. DAI/8909/84

CA 962

A Certificate of Validity

To renew a Certificate of Validity, and so the currency of the Permit to Fly, the aircraft must be inspected by an authorised inspector and then check flown by an authorised check pilot, (the inspector and check pilot can be the same person). The inspector, check pilot and owner complete an application form for the issue of a new Certificate of Validity.

The Certificate of Validity is issued by an organisation on behalf of the CAA. That organisation is usually the British Microlight Aircraft Association (BMAA), or the Popular Flying Association (PFA). The aircraft may not be flown until the new Certificate is received by the owner.

The Permit to Fly will be subject to operating conditions. These conditions are listed on the back of the Permit document. In essence, the standard operating conditions are:

- The aircraft may not be flown for aerial work other than instruction and testing of pilots for the issue or renewal of a licence or rating. The instructor and student or candidate must be members of the same club and the aircraft must be operated by that club. An aerial work flight is defined as a flight for which money is requested or promised.
- There is a further restriction on the use of some microlights for training. Kit or home-built microlights may only be used for the training of the sole owner of the aircraft (or their immediate family) if the student pays for the training in the aircraft. If the aircraft is owned by more than one person none of the owners, nor any other person, may be trained in the aircraft if payment is made for the training.

  Certain kits are Approved Kits produced simply for assembly by the owner and are not subject to this restriction.

  The logic behind the restriction is to protect the student pilot who is not the builder of the aircraft, if there is any possibility that the airworthiness state of the aircraft, not having been produced by a CAA-approved company, is not up to an acceptable standard. It is assumed that the builder will be prepared to accept any such risk

Conditions on a Permit to Fly

UNITED KINGDOM
CIVIL AVIATION AUTHORITY

Page 1 of 1

Dated: 11 OCTOBER 2004 CONDITIONS OF PERMIT TO FLY NO PR 051324/002

Nationality and Registration Marks	Constructor and Constructor's Designation of Aircraft	Aircraft Serial Number
G-EOFW	CYCLONE AIRSPORTS LTD TRADING AS PEGASUS AVIATION PEGASUS QUANTUM 15-912	7582

Where relevant, the Conditions associated with this Permit supersede those specified in the manufacturers' operating limitations.

1. The aircraft shall not be flown over any assembly of persons or over any congested area of a city, town or settlement, except to the extent necessary in order to take off and land at a Government or a licensed aerodrome in accordance with normal aviation practice.
2. The aircraft shall be maintained in an airworthy condition.
3. The aircraft shall be operated in accordance with the current procedures and limitations contained in the applicable technical publications and with the manufacturers' instructions for the type and model of aircraft.
4. The aircraft is permitted to fly only for non-aerobatic operation. Non-aerobatic operation includes:
   (i) any manoeuvre necessary for normal flying.
   (ii) intentional stalls from level flight.
   (iii) steep turns in which the angle of bank does not exceed 60 degrees.
5. Smoking in the aircraft is prohibited.
6. This aircraft is hereby granted a permission to fly for the purposes of aerial work which consists of the giving of instruction in flying or the conducting of flying tests subject to the aeroplane being owned or operated under arrangements entered into by a flying club of which the person giving the instruction or conducting the test and the person receiving the instruction or undergoing the test are both members.

for the Civil Aviation Authority

No entries or endorsements may be made on this document except by an authorised person.
960MS (Type Approved Microlight Aircraft)

- The aircraft may not be flown over any assembly of persons or the congested area of a city, town or settlement except that the aircraft can be flown over the congested area of a city, town or settlement when landing and taking-off at a Government or licensed aerodrome, but must be able to glide clear of that area in the event of an engine failure.
- The aircraft must be operated in accordance with any technical publications and operating procedures required by the manufacturer of the aircraft.
- The aircraft shall be maintained in an airworthy condition.
- The aircraft may not fly aerobatics or make any turn at over 60° angle of bank. Intentional stalls from level flight are not considered aerobatic.
- No smoking in the aircraft.

You should check the conditions listed on the back of the Permit for an aircraft you are going to fly for the full detailed wording.

▶ De-regulated Microlights

In April 2007 the CAA issued an exemption which allows microlight aircraft that are single seat aircraft with a maximum dry weight (without fuel or pilot) of 115 kilogrammes and have a maximum wing loading at maximum dry weight of 10 Kilogrammes per square metre to be operated without complying to any airworthiness requirements. This means the aircraft do not need a Permit to Fly or annual inspection. The aircraft are required to be registered and must carry a noise certificate. The pilot of such an aircraft must have a licence which entitles them to fly microlight aircraft and must carry third party insurance.

▶ Aircraft Equipment

There are certain minimum requirements for equipment required to be carried in aircraft. The requirements vary depending on the type of aircraft and the nature of the flight. The requirements for microlights are very simple.

Charts For all flights a pilot must carry a current chart of the area that you intend to fly over with details of the airspace up to the level to which it is intended to fly. Charts have a validity period of approximately one year. To ensure that your chart is current check the edition number printed on the chart against the list of current charts published in the green AIC.

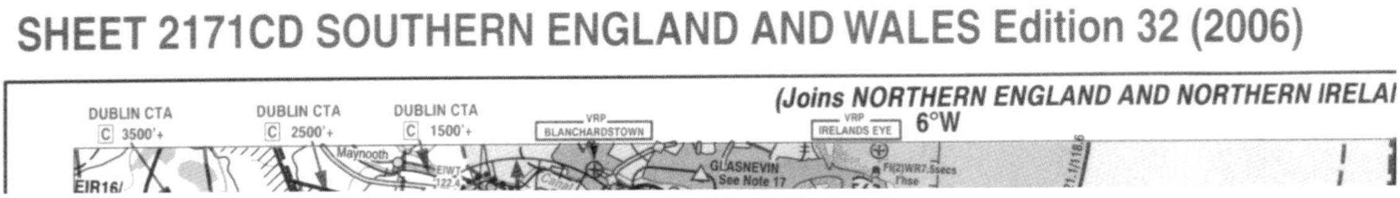

chart edition number

Transponders For flights above Flight Level 100 (FL100) the aircraft must be equipped with a transponder (the term Flight Level is described more fully later, but for now FL100 can be thought of as 10,000ft). When activated by a ground based radar signal, a transponder transmits a four number code which identifies the aircraft on a radar screen. Some transponders also transmit height information. There are several standard transponder codes;

- 7700 is the code for a Mayday. The code signifies that the aircraft is in distress and requires assistance.
- 7600 is the code used to transmit to controllers that an aircraft has suffered a radio failure.
- 7500 is used to inform controllers that the aircraft is the subject of unlawful interference, (hijack). Unlikely to be a problem on our aircraft.
- 7000 is the conspicuity code set by aircraft wishing to be highlighted on radar even when not using a radar service.

Instruments As part of the build requirements, all microlight aircraft must be fitted with an airspeed indicator and an altimeter. Particular manufacturers may require other instrumentation to be fitted to an individual aircraft type.

A transponder

▶ Aircraft Logbook 

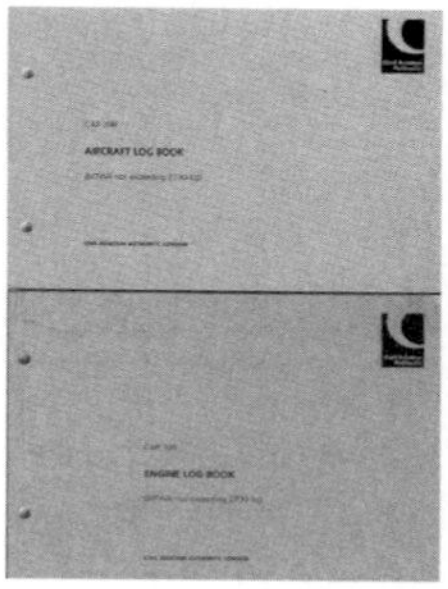

Aircraft and engine logbooks

The operator of a microlight aircraft or gyroplane must keep a logbook for the aircraft detailing the flight operating hours, aircraft maintenance, the engine operating hours, engine maintenance, modifications and work carried out.

The logbook forms part of the aircraft. The logbook must be kept for at least two years after the aircraft is destroyed or permanently withdrawn from use.

It is an offence in law to destroy a logbook with intent to deceive, or to make false entries or material omissions in the logbook.

▶ Radio Licence

WIRELESS TELEGRAPHY ACTS 1949 and 1998

Aeronautical Transportable Radio Licence

Ofcom

A radio licence

Aircraft may carry radios which can receive and transmit on aeronautical frequencies. The radio may be used to talk to ground stations for information purposes and also to communicate with ATC control or radar services. The radio is not to be used as an air-to-air chat line.

The aircraft radio must be licensed with the Civil Aviation Authority.

▶ Radio Operator's Licence

To operate the radio the pilot must hold a current Flight Radiotelephony Operators Licence (FRTOL). The FRTOL is achieved by passing a written examination and practical radio simulator test with an Authorised Radiotelephony Examiner. Details of examiners may be found on the CAA website.

A student pilot may operate the aircraft radio whilst under training without holding an FRTOL.

The FRTOL is usually issued to be valid for the life of the holder's licence. The UK PPL and PPL (M) were lifetime licences, as is the NPPL, however the FRTOL issued with them is valid for a maximum period of 10 years. UK-issued JAA (Joint Aviation Authority) PPLs are reissued every five years and so an FRTOL with a JAA PPL is reissued at the same time.

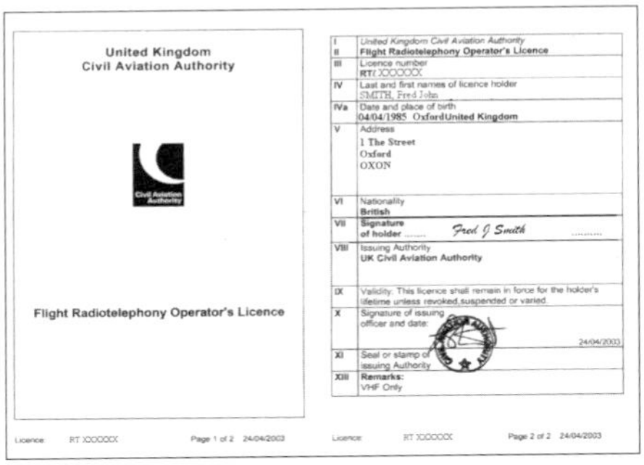
United Kingdom
Civil Aviation Authority
Civil Aviation Authority
Flight Radiotelephony Operator's Licence
Licence: RT XXXXXX Page 1 of 2 24/04/2003

I	United Kingdom Civil Aviation Authority
II	Flight Radiotelephony Operator's Licence
III	Licence number RT/ XXXXXX
IV	Last and first names of licence holder SMITH, Fred John
IVa	Date and place of birth 04/04/1985 Oxford United Kingdom
V	Address 1 The Street Oxford OXON
VI	Nationality British
VII	Signature of holder .... Fred J Smith ....
VIII	Issuing Authority UK Civil Aviation Authority
IX	Validity: This licence shall remain in force for the holder's lifetime unless revoked, suspended or varied.
X	Signature of issuing officer and date: 24/04/2003
XI	Seal or stamp of issuing Authority
XIII	Remarks: VHF Only

Licence: RT XXXXXX Page 2 of 2 24/04/2003

A FRTOL (both sides)

The FRTOL is only valid for use with aircraft radios and is not valid for the use of ground-based stations or hand-held radios not fitted to aircraft. An additional qualification is required to operate these ground radios.

Where a radio operator's licence is issued for use only with ground-based radios it will have a validity period of 10 years.

At present there is no fee for the issue of a FRTOL to holders of existing pilot's licences or applicants for the initial grant of a pilot's licence. There is a fee for the grant of a radio licence for a ground operator.

▶ Revision

42 With certain exceptions all powered aircraft flying in the UK are required to be registered. Correct registration of the aircraft is the responsibility of:

A The pilot

B The CAA

C The owner

D The operator

43 When the aircraft is owned by more than one person the minimum share that any one owner may hold is:

A 1%

B 5%

C 10%

D 15%

44 Microlights are operated on a Permit To Fly airworthiness document. The Permit must have a current Certificate of Validity to be in force. The Certificate of Validity is valid for:

A 6 months

B 12 months

C 13 months

D 2 years

45 The Permit to Fly is subject to certain conditions, which usually include:

A Prohibiting all flight over built up areas at all times

B Prohibiting aerobatics including all intentional stalls

C Prohibiting all flying with passengers

D Prohibiting smoking in the aircraft

46 All microlight aircraft must maintain an engine and aircraft logbook. The logbook:

A Must be kept for at least two years after the date of the last entry

B Must be retained by the owner after the aircraft is sold to prevent fraud

C Must be submitted to the CAA after any substantial work has been carried out on the aircraft

D Must be kept with the aircraft until the aircraft is destroyed or permanently withdrawn from use

Answers on page 169

Aircraft Operation

Aircraft Operation

- ▶ Towing
- ▶ Launching, Picking up and Dropping of Tow Ropes at Aerodromes
- ▶ Dropping Articles from Aircraft
- ▶ Lights on Aircraft
- ▶ Carriage of Weapons and Munitions of War
- ▶ Carriage of Dangerous Goods
- ▶ Method of Carriage of Persons
- ▶ Revision

▶ Towing

An aircraft may not tow gliders or any other object behind it without having a modification which is approved for the purpose. Each particular aircraft fitted with a towing modification must be inspected and approved individually.

Aircraft towing other aircraft or gliders are considered to be one aircraft under the command of the commander of the towing aircraft.

▶ Launching, Picking up and Dropping of Tow Ropes at Aerodromes

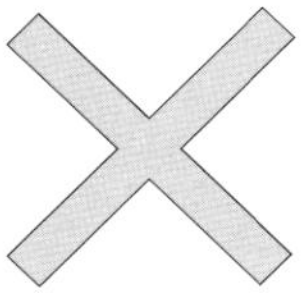

Tow ropes, banners, or similar articles towed by an aircraft must not be launched, picked up or dropped at an aerodrome except in accordance with arrangements made with an air traffic control unit at the aerodrome, or if there is no such unit, with the person in charge of the aerodrome.

When dropping tow ropes at an airfield, the dropping is usually done in an area marked with a yellow cross, and with the aircraft flying in the direction of take-off and landing.

▶ Dropping Articles from Aircraft

Except in an emergency, nothing may be dropped from an aircraft in flight with the exception of ballast in the form of fine sand or water. It is possible to get exemptions from this rule for activities such as flour bombing competitions.

No person shall drop from an aircraft in flight except with the written permission of the CAA – obviously this chiefly concerns the activity of parachuting. Dropping includes projecting and lowering.

▶ Lights on Aircraft

An anti-collision light

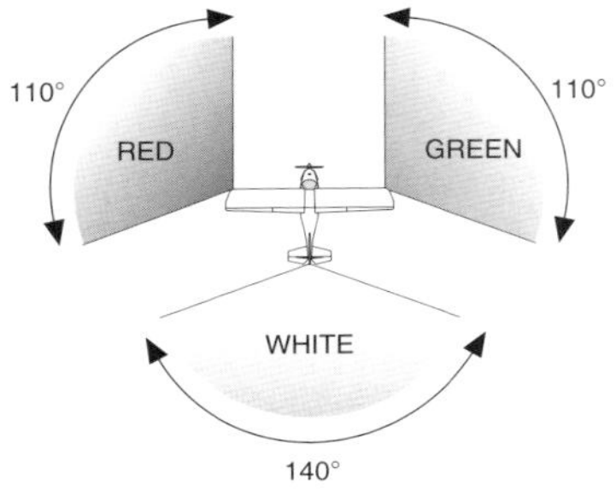

Navigation lights

There are no requirements for aircraft flying during the day to be equipped with any lights.

You may choose to fit an anti-collision light to your aircraft. This light may be a flashing red or white light which will make you visible in all directions.

Conventional aircraft may be fitted with navigation lights. Knowing the arc of these lights helps you to assess the direction of movement of the aircraft and so decide whether any risk of collision exists.

The right-hand (green)...

and left-hand (red) navigation lights

The rear white navigation light

The navigation lights on the right wing of the aircraft will be green and show through an arc of 110° from dead ahead. The navigation lights on the left wing of the aircraft will be red and show through an arc of 110° from dead ahead.

At the rear of the aircraft will be a white light showing through 140°.

▶ Carriage of Weapons and Munitions of War

Munitions of war may only be carried with the permission of the CAA. Weapons, munitions of war and their component parts must not be carried in any part of the aircraft accessible to passengers. Firearms must be unloaded.

▶ Carriage of Dangerous Goods

Certain goods are classified as dangerous. Those dangerous goods permitted to be carried in an aircraft are subject to special conditions of handling, loading, packing, labelling and documentation. Classification lists and conditions are published in the form of regulations made from time to time by the Secretary of State. As a commonsense practice, private pilots should make a habit of checking anything being carried in their aircraft for dangerous items – eg certain types of matches and lighters.

Although not a dangerous goods item, pilots should be aware that mobile telephones should be switched off when carried in an aircraft. Their transmitting can cause interference to radio and navigation equipment carried on the aircraft and to the ground aerial system. Details are currently in AIC 1/2004 (Pink 62) issued in 2004.

▶ Method of Carriage of Persons

No one must be in, or on, any part of an aircraft in flight which is not designed for the accommodation of people. Nor can a person be in, or on, any object (other than a glider or flying machine), towed or attached to an aircraft in flight except for temporary access to any part of the aircraft for the purpose of taking action necessary for the safety of the aircraft or any person on board.

▶ Revision

47 Without a transponder fitted to the aircraft no flight is allowed above a certain level except with the permission of and Air Traffic Control unit. That level is:

A 100,000 feet

B Flight Level 80

C Flight Level 100

D Flight Level 245

48 The Rules of the Air require an aircraft to always carry which item when flying VFR in the UK?

A A chart

B A direction indicator

C A transponder

D A radio

49 Where an aircraft is fitted with a radio which of the following is true?

A The radio needs to be licensed and the operator, unless a student under training, requires a licence to use the radio

B The radio needs to be licensed and the operator, even a student under training, requires a licence to use the radio

C The radio installation does not need a licence but the operator does

D The radio only needs a licence if it is fitted into the aircraft

50 Munitions of war maybe carried in an aircraft:

A Never

B With the permission of the CAA

C Only for flight remaining within 8nm of the departure airfield

D Provided they belong to the pilot

51 Which of the following is true?

A Any aircraft may be used for towing without any requirement for modification or permission

B Aircraft to be used for towing must be individually inspected and approved and operated within the approval

C An aircraft may be used for towing without having to apply for an individual permission if another aircraft of the same type has already been cleared for towing

D Only aircraft with a Certificate of Airworthiness may be used for towing

52 When dropping tow ropes at an aerodrome the aircraft should:

A Fly in the opposite direction to take-off to make it obvious what he or she is doing

B Drop the rope outside the aerodrome boundary

C Fly in the same direction as the take-off

D Land with the rope still attached so that it cannot land accidentally on another aircraft

53 A tow rope dropping area is marked by which symbol?

A A red cross

B A double white cross

C An orange circle

D A yellow cross

---

54 Which articles may be dropped from an aircraft in flight without a special permission?

A Water ballast

B Wind indicators

C Flour bombs

D Parachutists

Answers on page 169

Visual
Flight Rules
(Rules 24-27)

Visual Flight Rules (Rules 24-27)

- Visual Flight Rules
- Revision

▶ Visual Flight Rules

The Visual Flight Rules (VFR), allow flight in compliance with specified visibility and cloud clearance minima. The minima vary depending on the airspace classification, the level at which the flight is to be conducted and the speed at which the aircraft is to be flown. The minima are called the Visual Meteorological Conditions (VMC).

As a condition of the Permit to Fly, many types of aircraft can only fly in accordance with the Visual Flight Rules, and therefore within the VMC minima set out in the following table. Although the VMC minima allow flight in a visibility of 1500 metres in some cases, the NPPL licence privileges restrict the holder to an in-flight visibility of at least 3km. This greater minimum visibility will always take priority over the 1500 metre VMC minimum.

At the time of writing the privileges of the PPL Gyroplanes and PPL Balloons do not restrict visibility any further than VMC minima. There is, however, a proposal to add a restriction to the PPL Gyroplanes and PPL Helicopters restricting pilots to flight in visibility of 3 kilometres or greater and to remain within sight of the surface at all times.

Refer to the table below for the VMC minima in different classes of airspace for flight at airspeeds no faster than 140 knots indicated. Airspace classes are explained shortly:

	Class A	Class B, C, D, E	Class F, G
FL100 and above	VFR not permitted unless as Special VFR if airspace is a Zone	Cloud clearance: 1000 feet vertically and 1500m horizontally. Min visibility: 8km	Cloud clearance: 1000 feet vertically and 1500m horizontally. Min visibility: 8km
Below FL100 and above 3000ft Above Mean Sea Level		Cloud clearance: 1000 feet vertically and 1500m horizontally. Min visibility: 5km	Cloud clearance: 1000 feet vertically and 1500m horizontally. Min visibility: 5km
3000ft Above Mean Sea Level and below		Cloud clearance: Clear of cloud, within sight of the surface. Min visibility: 5km	Cloud clearance: Clear of cloud, within sight of the surface. Min visibility: 1500m

When determining visibility for flight within Class D controlled airspace, the controller (not the pilot) is responsible for determining the visibility for flights taking-off from and landing within the airspace. The pilot is responsible for determining flight visibility for transit flights passing through class D airspace and when flying outside class D airspace.

▶ Revision

55 Visual flight rules require that an aircraft is flown in accordance with the Visual Meteorological Conditions (VMC) minima. Which of the following statements is correct?

A The VMC minima dictate minimum requirements of in flight visibility and aircraft separation from cloud for all classes of airspace

B The VMC minima dictate minimum requirements of in flight visibility and aircraft separation from cloud for flight outside controlled airspace only

C The VMC minima dictate minimum requirements of in flight visibility and aircraft separation from cloud for flight inside controlled airspace only

D The VMC minima dictate minimum requirements of in flight visibility and aircraft separation from cloud for all classes of airspace for aircraft flying at or below 140 knots true air speed only

56 When transiting class D airspace (but not taking off or landing), in order to calculate VMC minima, visibility is determined by:

A The ATC controller

B Meteorological observation at the controlling airfield

C The pilot

D The authorising instructor

Answers on page 169

Airspace

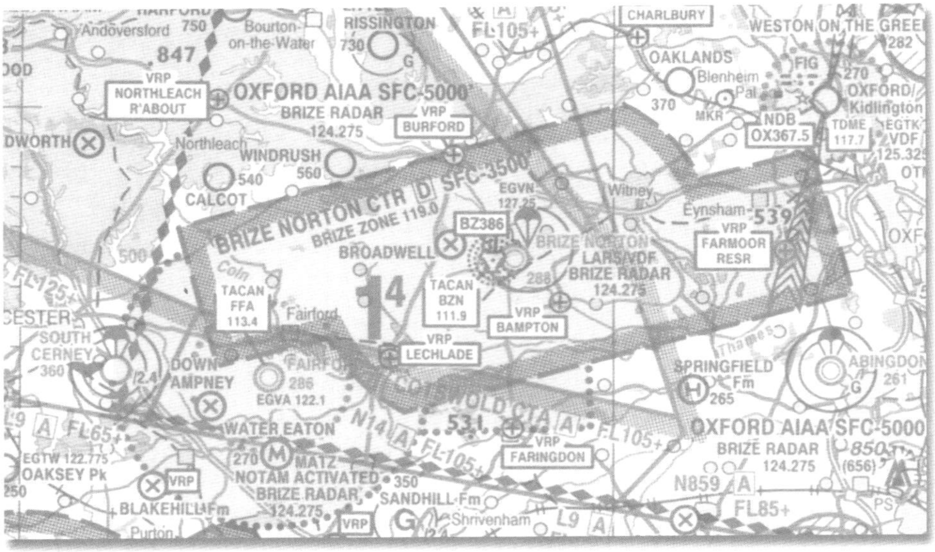
Andoversford
750
Bourton-on-the-Water
RISSINGTON
730
FL105+
CHARLBURY
WESTON ON THE GREEN
282
847
VRP
NORTHLEACH R'ABOUT
OXFORD AIAA SFC-5000'
BRIZE RADAR 124.275
VRP BURFORD
OAKLANDS
Blenheim Pal
FIG
270
OXFORD Kidlington
370
MKR
NDB OX367.5
TDME 117.7
EGTK VDF
Northleach
WINDRUSH 560
540
CALCOT
EGVN 127.25
Witney
Eynsham
539
BRIZE NORTON CTR D SFC-3500'
BRIZE ZONE 119.0
BZ386
BRIZE NORTON
LARS/VDF BRIZE RADAR 124.275
VRP FARMOOR RESR
BROADWELL
500
Coln
TACAN FFA 113.4
Fairford
TACAN BZN 111.9
288
VRP BAMPTON
SOUTH CERNEY
360
DOWN AMPNEY
VRP LECHLADE
Thames
SPRINGFIELD Fm
265
ABINGDON
261
286
EGVA 122.1
COTSWOLD CTA
531
FL65+
WATER EATON
N14
FL105+
VRP FARINGDON
OXFORD AIAA SFC-5000
BRIZE RADAR 124.275
850
(656)
EGTW 122.775
OAKSEY Pk
270
MATZ
NOTAM ACTIVATED
350
BRIZE RADAR 124.275
N859
FL85+
250
VRP
BLAKEHILL Fm
SANDHILL Fm
Shrivenham
L9
Purton
VRP

Airspace

- National Airspace Boundary
- Controlled Airspace
- Airspace Classification
- Flight in Class A Airspace
- Types of Airspace
- Aerodrome Traffic Zones (ATZ)
- Visual Signals at Aerodromes
- Military Aerodrome Traffic Zones – MATZ
- Aerodrome Beacons
- Revision

▶ National Airspace Boundary

UK airspace is divided into Flight Information Regions (FIR). The external boundary of these regions can be thought of as the edge of UK national airspace.

The London, Scottish and Shannon FIR boundaries

Lower airspace (below FL 245, or approximately 24,500ft) in the UK comprises of two regions known as the London and Scottish Flight Information Regions (FIR).

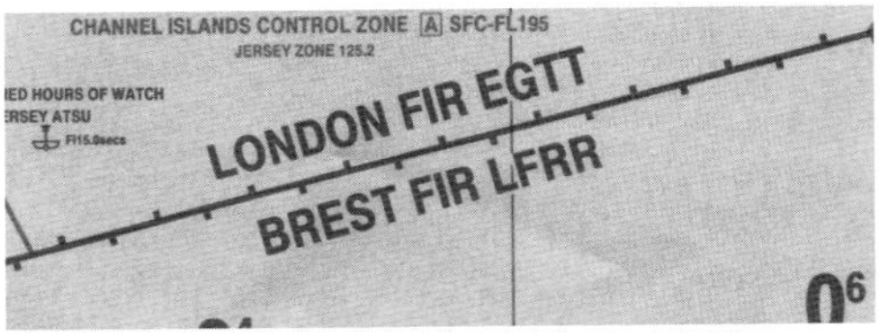

A section of the London FIR boundary as depicted on the 1:500,000 aeronautical chart

Upper airspace (at and above FL 245) in the UK comprises of the same two geographic regions, known as the London and Scottish Upper Flight Information Regions (UIR). The upper level of the UIR is FL 660 (approximately 66,000ft)

▶ Controlled Airspace

In common with international protocols, UK airspace is divided into 'controlled' and 'uncontrolled' airspace.

Flight within controlled airspace requires an air traffic control clearance before entry. It is not the purpose of controlled airspace to restrict activity, but to ensure that activity within it is safely carried out.

To enter controlled airspace a clearance, permission, is required from the controlling authority and the flight must be conducted in accordance with any specified clearances or conditions.

It is the duty of the commander of an aircraft to ensure that he or she can comply with any clearance before accepting it and before entering controlled airspace. If a clearance cannot be complied with, the commander of the aircraft must make that clear to the controlling authority right away.

The controlling authority does not have to know the licences and limitations of the pilot or the aircraft type to give a clearance, and so it is the responsibility of the commander to make sure that the clearance can be legally complied with before accepting it.

▶ Airspace Classification

Airspace is further classified as a 'Class' of airspace between A and G. A, B, C, D and E are all classes of controlled airspace. In class E airspace only Instrument Flight Rule traffic is controlled, Visual Flight Rule traffic is not. Class F and G airspace is uncontrolled for all classes of traffic.

Aeronautical charts show the airspace classification by printing a letter to signify the class next to the airspace identity and by using different boundary line patterns around the edge of the airspace.

▶ Flight in Class A Airspace

Flight in Class A airspace must be conducted under Instrument Flight Rules (IFR) regardless of the actual weather conditions. Many aircraft are restricted to flight only in compliance with Visual Flight Rules (VFR), and so these aircraft cannot fly in Class A airspace – with one exception.

A special flight clearance for flight in Class A airspace which is a control zone may be granted at the discretion of the controller. The minimum flight visibility will normally be 10 kilometres and the aircraft must remain clear of cloud and in sight of the surface. This clearance is known as a Special Visual Flight Rule clearance, SVFR.

For flights to aerodromes within a Class A control zone, local arrangements may be in place which allow SVFR flight in visibility less than 10 kilometres by the holders of some licences. However, the NPPL holder is always restricted to a minimum visibility of 10km on a SVFR clearance even where such local arrangements exist. Details of these procedures will be found in the Aerodrome section of the Aeronautical Information Publication (AIP).

▶ Types of Airspace

Control Zone

Controlled airspace in the form of a Control Zone extends from ground level to a specified altitude or flight level. On an aeronautical chart a control zone will be labelled as 'CTR'.

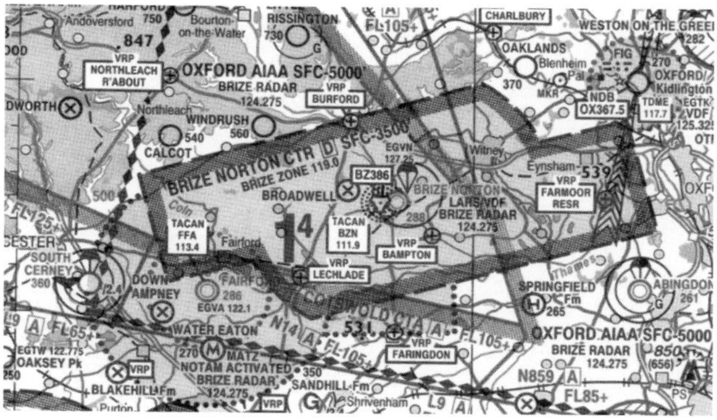

The Brize Norton control zone as depicted on a 1:500,000 aeronautical chart. The outer boundary is a broken line with shading on the inside. The zone extends from the surface to 3,500 feet above mean sea level (AMSL), indicated by 'SFC-3500' Class D airspace. The zone radio frequency is 119.00

Control Area

Controlled airspace in the form of a Control Area extends from a specified altitude or flight level to another altitude or flight level. On an aeronautical chart the control area will be labelled as 'CTA'.

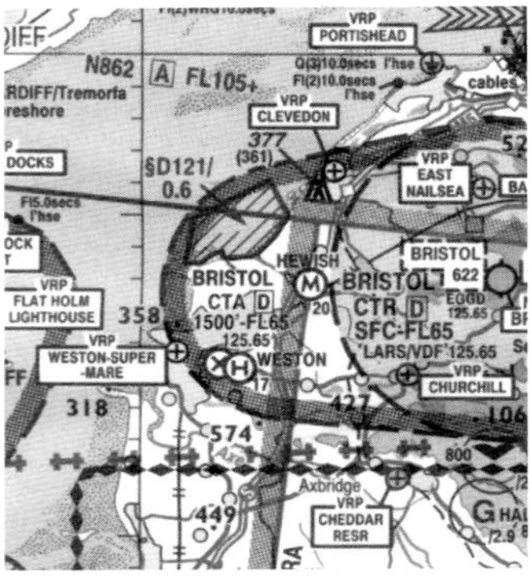

Part of the Bristol control area as depicted on a 1:500,000 aeronautical chart. The airspace is class D and extends from 1500ft amsl to FL65. The adjoining control zone (CTR) is from the surface to FL65

Terminal Control Area

Controlled airspace in the area of one or more major aerodromes in the form of a very large control area into which aircraft from the aerodromes will be fed for overall control of the airspace overlapping the aerodromes. It is common for several airways (flight corridors) to link into this large area which is called a Terminal Control Area and on an aeronautical chart will be labelled as 'TMA'.

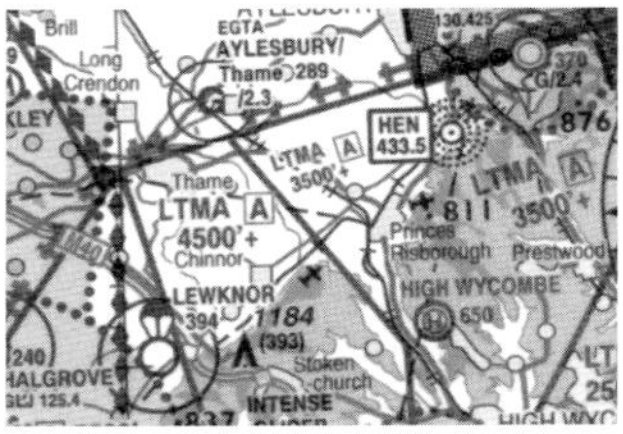

A corner of the London Terminal Control Area as depicted on a 1:500,000 aeronautical chart. The centre section labelled 'LTMA' (London TMA) is Class A airspace and extends from 4500ft amsl to FL195, indicated by the "+" on this series of charts

Airway

Controlled airspace in the form of an airway is a control area aligned as a corridor with a standard width of 10 nautical miles. The centre line of the airway is often aligned on radio navigation beacons. Each airway has a letter and number identification and the upper and lower limits of the airway are marked on aeronautical navigation charts. The airways have a lower limit that tends to lower where the airway is nearer to the aerodromes it serves to allow aircraft climbing or descending to do so in controlled airspace.

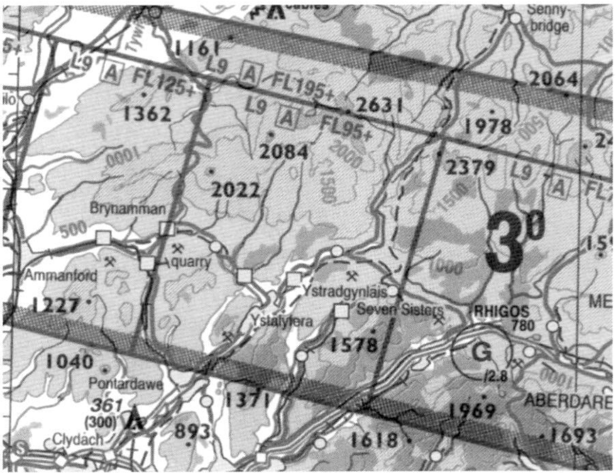

A section of an airway as depicted on a 1:500,000 aeronautical chart. The centre section labelled L9 is Class A airspace and extends from FL95 to FL195, indicated by the plus sign, '+', on this series of charts

Advisory airspace

Some airspace within the UK comprises of Air Traffic Service advisory routes. These are corridors of advisory airspace similar to airways but outside controlled airspace, the airspace is classified Class F. Aircraft using the separation services within the advisory route are advised of other aircraft doing the same but it must be remembered that it is not a mandatory service and other aircraft not using the service may be in the airspace too. An Air Traffic Advisory Service is provided to participating flights and to this extent the air traffic control is advisory because it is not mandatory to comply with the instructions from the air traffic control unit, but pilots are assumed to be doing so unless they state otherwise.

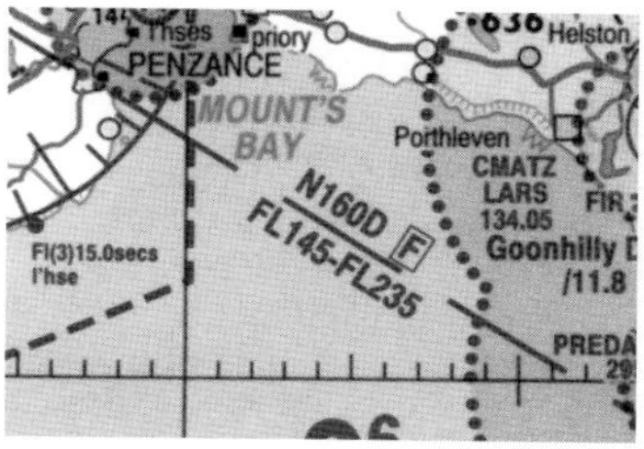

A section of Class F airspace as depicted on the 1:500,000 aeronautical chart. This particular section, N160D, has a lower limit of FL145 and an upper limit of FL235

Uncontrolled airspace

As the name implies, all that outside controlled or advisory airspace is uncontrolled airspace. Subject to airspace restrictions described later, flight in uncontrolled airspace requires no prior permission, no air traffic control service and – mostly – no need to speak to anybody at all.

▶Aerodrome Traffic Zones (ATZ)

An Aerodrome Traffic Zone (ATZ) is the airspace at specific aerodromes within which the regulations contained in Rule 39 apply.

Aerodromes Traffic Zones adopt the class of the airspace within which they are located. Flight within the aerodrome's traffic zone are subject to the Rule 39 requirements, but where the requirements of a particular airspace class are more stringent they take precedence.

An ATZ extends vertically from the surface to 2000 feet above aerodrome level (AAL). If the longest runway is 1850m or less the zone is the area within a circle of 2 nautical miles radius centred on the runway midpoint.

If this zone does not extend at least 1·5 nautical miles beyond the end of any runway, or if the longest runway is more than 1850m long, the radius of the ATZ is 2·5 nautical miles.

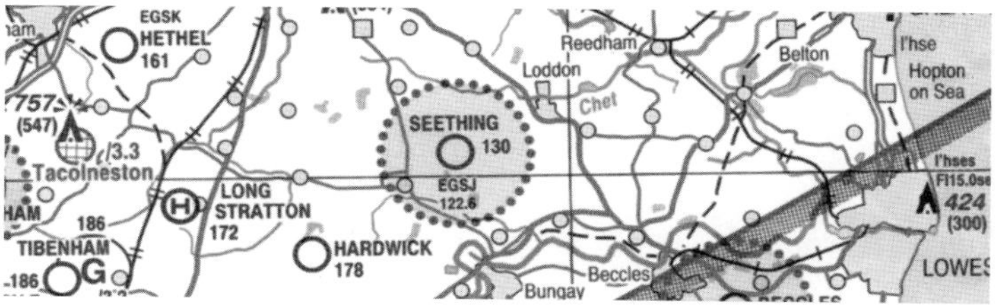

An ATZ as shown on a 1:500,000 aeronautical chart. The aerodrome is SEETHING and the aerodrome elevation is 130 feet above mean sea level, AMSL

An Aerodrome Traffic Zone at a civilian airfield is active during the notified hours of watch of the air traffic service unit at the aerodrome. Details of these hours of watch can be found in the Aerodromes section of the Aeronautical Information Publication.

Aircraft wishing to fly through an ATZ must, prior to entry, communicate with the air traffic service at the aerodrome and establish sufficient information to enable flight within the zone to be conducted safely. Aircraft flying within the zone must conform to any existing traffic pattern, or keep clear of the airspace in which that pattern of traffic is formed.

Flights entering the zone must give their position and height to the air traffic service at the aerodrome on the radio frequency notified for use.

When flying through an ATZ the pilot must maintain a continuous watch on the appropriate radio frequency notified for communications at the aerodrome or, if this is not possible, keep a watch for visual instructions.

Flights leaving the ATZ must give their position and height to the air traffic service at the aerodrome on the radio frequency notified for use.

▶Visual Signals at Aerodromes

An aircraft on, or in the traffic pattern at, an aerodrome must comply with visual signals made by the aerodrome authorities. The commander of an aircraft does not have to obey marshalling signals if they seem unsafe.

▶Military Aerodrome Traffic Zones – MATZ

Some military airfields are situated within controlled airspace or have their own Control Zone – CTR. Others are outside controlled airspace and have an ATZ of the same size as a civil aerodrome. Some military aerodromes have an additional larger zone around the ATZ, within which military aircraft regularly operate. This larger zone is called a Military Aerodrome Traffic Zone (MATZ) and is usually of standard dimensions.

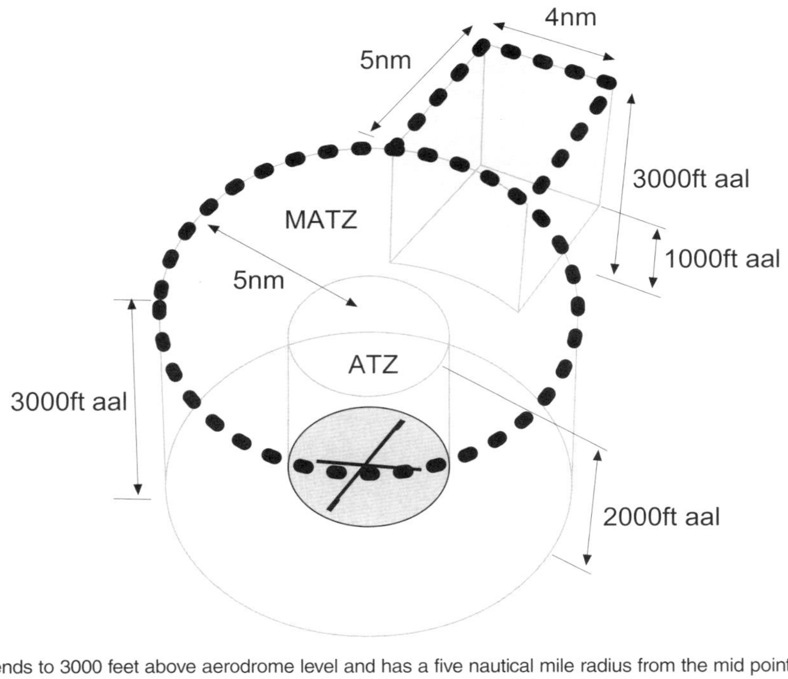

A standard MATZ extends to 3000 feet above aerodrome level and has a five nautical mile radius from the mid point of the longest runway

Most MATZ have an extended corridor of a further 5 nautical miles lined up with the main runway, this corridor has a width of 4 nautical miles. These extensions, commonly known as 'stubs' or 'pan handles', have vertical limits from1000 feet above aerodrome level to 3000 feet above aerodrome level. Therefore, depending upon the terrain it may be possible to fly under a MATZ stub without being in the MATZ.

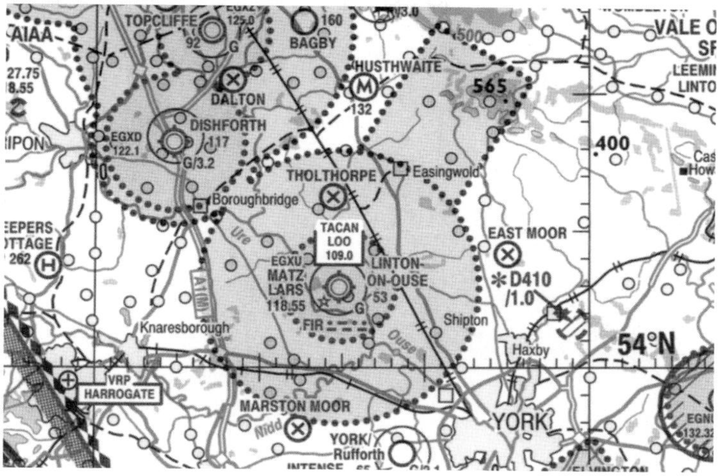

The tinted area is a MATZ as depicted on a 1:500,000 aeronautical chart. The ATZ can be seen inside the MATZ boundaries

When two or more MATZ overlap, the entire combined zone (CMATZ), will be controlled by one authority. The upper limit of the whole of the airspace in the zone will be 3000 feet above the highest of the aerodromes within the zone, whether or not that one is the controlling authority.

If you wish to fly within a MATZ you are strongly advised to do so under the control of the controlling authority – although legally the MATZ is not controlled airspace, although there will always be an ATZ within the MATZ which cannot be entered without permission. ATZs at military aerodromes are normally active 24 hours a day.

If you wish to enter a MATZ, you should establish communication with the MATZ controller when at least 15 miles or 5 minutes flying time (whichever is the greater), from the zone boundary. When making the initial call to the aerodrome the call should include the phrase 'request MATZ penetration'. The altimeter setting for a MATZ crossing will usually be the aerodrome QFE.

▶ Aerodrome Beacons

Location beacons displaying either flashing green and white or simply flashing white lights are provided at some aerodromes considered to be difficult to locate at night and during poor visibility.

Identification beacons are beacons which flash a two letter identification in Morse code every twelve seconds. Beacons at civil aerodromes are green and those at military aerodromes are red.

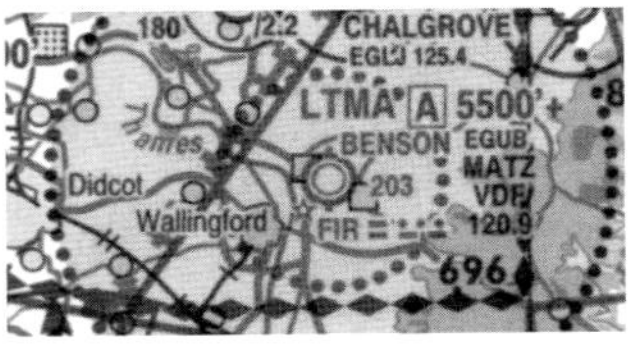

An Aerodrome Identification Beacon as depicted on a 1:500,000 aeronautical chart. The star shows that a beacon is present on the aerodrome. The letters FIR and the following dashes and dots tell that it is an identification beacon flashing the Morse letters for 'B O' in red

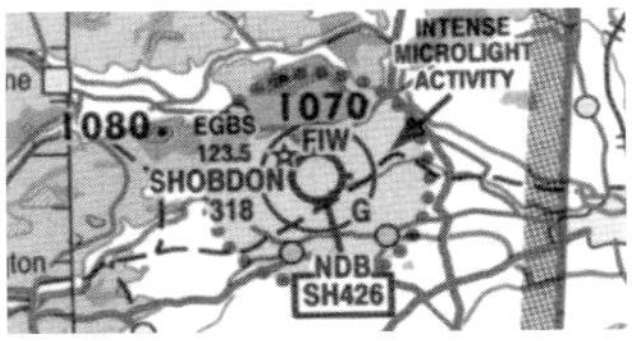

An Aerodrome Beacon as depicted on a 1:500,000 aeronautical chart. The star shows that a beacon is present on the aerodrome. The letters FIW show that it is just a flashing white light

▶ Revision

57 Airspace within the national boundary is divided into:

A National Upper and Lower airspace

B Internal Airspace

C Flight Information Regions

D Inner, Upper and Lower Airspace

58 The upper limit of the national airspace is:

A Flight Level 100

B Flight Level 245

C Flight Level 500

D Flight Level 660

59 Which of the following classes of airspace are classified as controlled airspace?

A A, B, C, D, E

B A, B, C, D

C A, B, C, D, E, F

D A, B, C, D, E, F, G

60 In which class of airspace may an aircraft not normally be flown under Visual Flight Rules?

A A

B B

C C

D D

61 The vertical limits of control zones are defined as:

A From the surface up to a height above ground level

B From the surface up to a height above aerodrome level

C From the surface to an altitude or flight level

D From an altitude or flight level to an altitude or flight level

62 The vertical limits of control areas are defined as:

A From the surface up to a height above ground level

B From the surface up to a height above aerodrome level

C From the surface to an altitude or flight level

D From an altitude or flight level to an altitude or flight level

63 A Terminal Control Area (TMA):

A Will serve one or more major airports

B Is the airspace at the end of each airway

C Forms part of the airway which it serves

D Is airspace which starts at the surface and reaches to the top of the Upper airspace

64 An Airway:

A Is reserved airspace into which only commercial flights are allowed

B Can be crossed at right angles by VFR traffic without them having to comply with airspace restrictions

C Is a control area in the form of a corridor

D Contains IFR and VFR traffic which must comply to the quadrantal or semi circular rule dependant on the level at which the aircraft is flying

---

65 Which class of airspace is established specifically in the form of a corridor to provide an Air Traffic Advisory Service to IFR flights?

A A

B C

C E

D F

---

66 An Aerodrome Traffic Zone (ATZ) has standard dimensions. These are:

A Height of 2000 feet above aerodrome level, radius 2 or 2·5 nautical miles from the runway midpoint

B Height of 3000 feet above aerodrome level, radius 2 or 2·5 nautical miles from the runway midpoint

C Height of 2000 feet above aerodrome level, radius 2 or 2·5 nautical miles from the airfield boundary

D Height of 3000 feet above aerodrome level, radius 2 or 2·5 nautical miles from the airfield boundary

---

67 A Military Aerodrome Traffic Zone (MATZ) is established at some military aerodromes. The normal size of a MATZ is

A Height of 2000 feet above aerodrome level, radius 2 or 2.5 nautical miles of the runway midpoint

B Height of 3000 feet above aerodrome level, radius 2 or 2.5 nautical miles of the runway midpoint

C Height of 3000 feet above aerodrome level, radius 5 nautical miles of the runway midpoint

D Height of 3000 feet above aerodrome level, radius 5 nautical miles of the airfield boundary

---

68 Flight within a MATZ will normally be conducted on which altimeter setting?

A Airfield QFE

B Airfield QNH

C Regional QNH

D Standard Altimeter Setting of 1013.2 millibars

---

69 The identification beacon at a military aerodrome will:

A Flash a 2 letter Morse signal in green every 12 seconds

B Flash a 2 letter Morse signal in white every 12 seconds

C Flash a 2 letter Morse signal in red every 12 seconds

D Flash an alternate green and white light every 30 seconds

Answers on page 170

Airspace Restrictions and Hazards

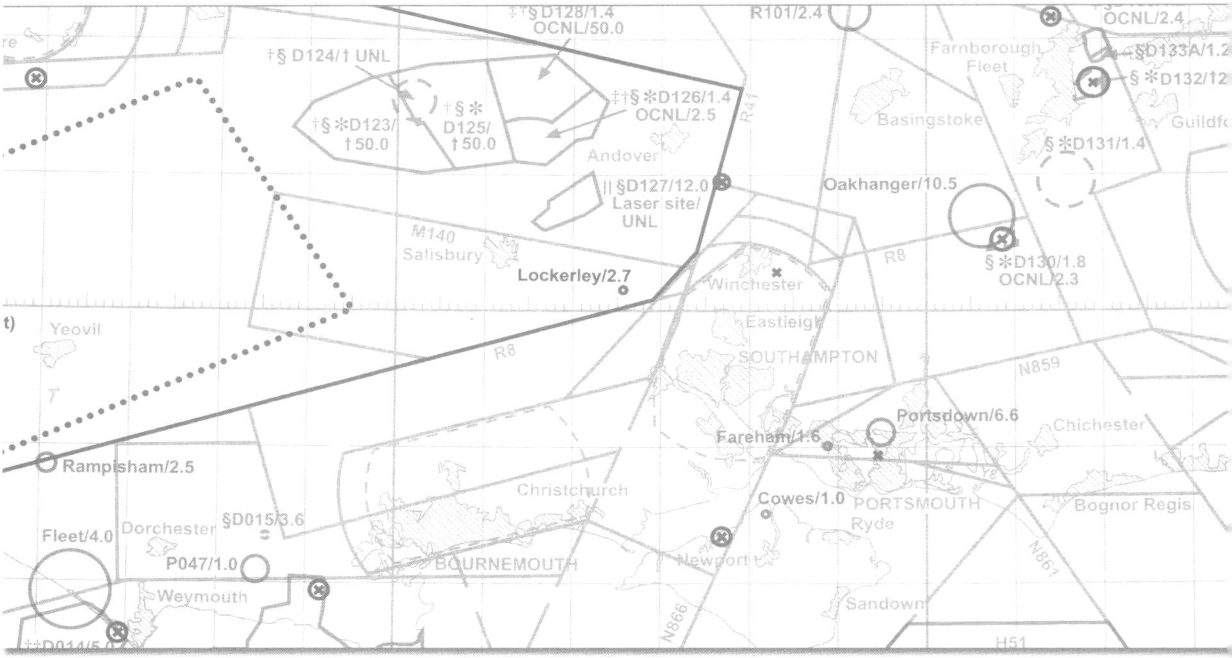

Airspace Restrictions and Hazards

- Charts
- Prohibited Area
- Restricted Area
- Danger Area
- Areas of Intensive Aerial Activity (AIAA)
- Military Low Flying
- Aerial Tactics Areas
- Military Training Areas (MTA) and Military Temporary Reserved Airspace (MTRA)
- Small Arms Ranges
- High Intensity Radio Transmission Area (HIRTA)
- Bird Hazards
- Hang Gliding, Paragliding and Parascending Sites
- Glider Launching
- Cable Launching Hang Gliders, Paragliders, Parascenders and Gliders
- Microlight Flying
- Balloon Launching
- Gas Venting Operations
- Free-fall Parachuting
- En-route Obstacles
- Flarestacks
- Hills and Mountains
- Revision

▶ Charts

The 'ENR' section of the UK AIP includes a 'Chart of United Kingdom Airspace Restrictions and Hazardous Areas' and a 'Chart of UK areas of Intensive Aerial Activity and Military Low Flying System'.

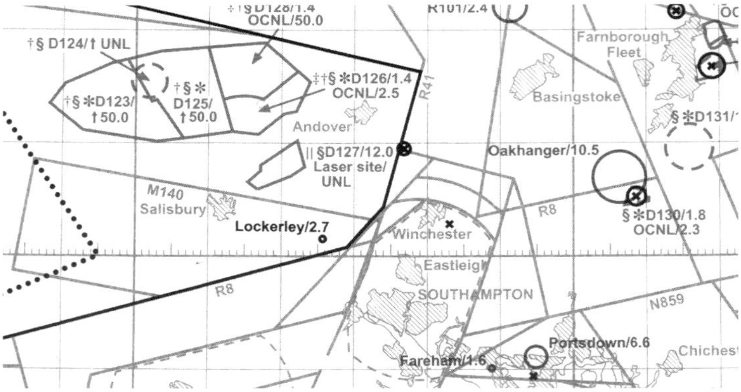

A section of the Chart of United Kingdom Airspace Restrictions:
Blue circle: High Intensity Radio Area
Green circle: Intense Bird activity area
Purple Circle P047: Prohibited area
Purple Circle R032: Restricted area
Black X in circle: Small Arms range
Solid red line: Scheduled Danger area
Pecked red line: Notified Danger area

Many of these areas are also shown on aeronautical charts used for in-flight navigation.

▶ Prohibited Area

Airspace of defined dimensions, extending up from the surface, within which flight is prohibited. The upper limit as shown on charts is an altitude (above mean sea level – amsl) based on the 'QNH' altimeter setting – explained in more detail later.

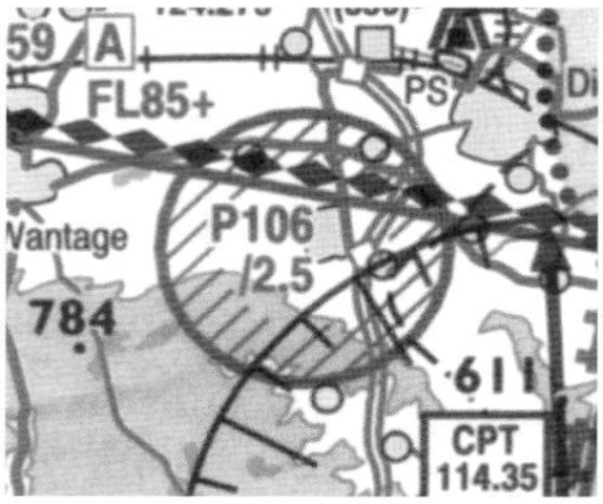

A prohibited area as depicted on a 1:500,000 aeronautical chart. This area is identified as P106 and noted as extending up to 2,500ft amsl

▶ Restricted Area

Airspace of defined dimensions within which flight is restricted in accordance with certain specified conditions. The conditions are usually noted in the chart legend 'notes' section. Many areas are restricted to prevent the flight of helicopters through them, some specifically exclude microlight aircraft. The upper limit as shown on charts is an altitude (based on the QNH).

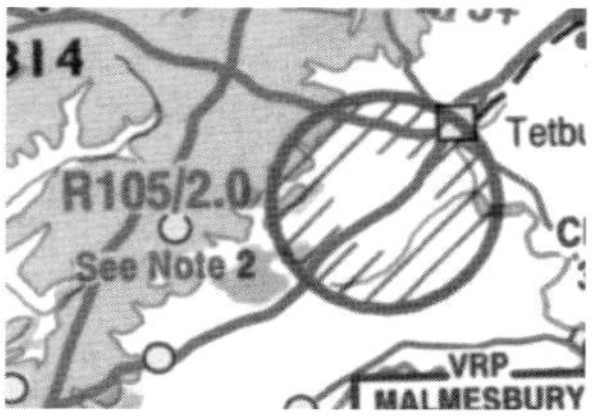

A restricted area as depicted on a 1:500,000 aeronautical chart. This area is identified as R105 and noted as extending up to 2000ft amsl. 'Note 2' refers to the detail of the restrictions as listed on the chart legend

▶ Danger Area

Airspace which has been notified as an area within which activities dangerous to the flight of aircraft may take place or exist, at such times as may be notified. The times of activity for these areas are listed on the 'Chart of United Kingdom Airspace Restrictions and Hazardous Areas' and also found in many commercial flight guides.

Danger areas are not prohibited or restricted areas by right, although flight within the airspace may endanger the aircraft and that is in itself an offence. Some danger areas are protected by local bylaws which prohibit entry during periods of activity. If an area is protected by bylaw the restriction will be shown on the Chart of United Kingdom Restrictions and Hazardous Areas, ENR 6-5-1-1, and on the legend of the 1:500,000 UK aeronautical chart.

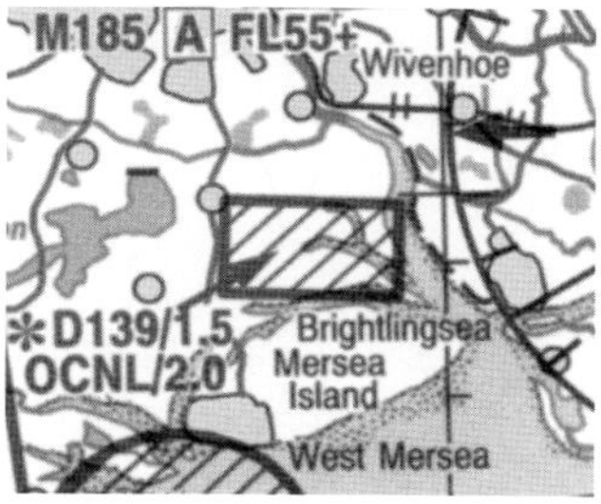

A scheduled danger area as depicted on a 1:500,000 aeronautical chart. This area is identified as D139 and noted extending to 1500ft amsl, with the upper limit raised occasionally to 2000ft amsl. The asterisk denotes that a bylaw prohibits entry during active hours

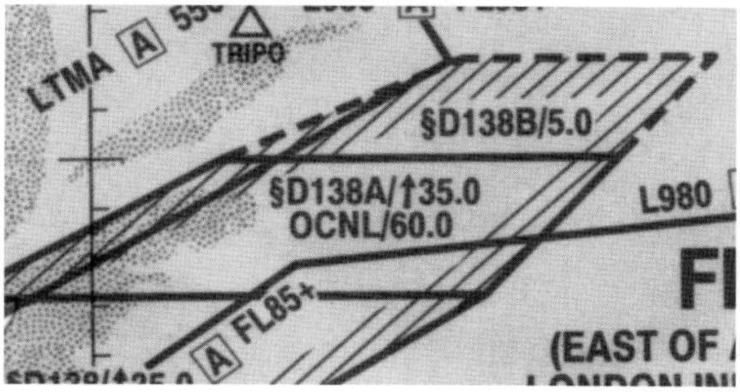

A notified danger area (as depicted by the pecked outline) on a 1:500,000 aeronautical chart. This area is identified as D138B and noted as extending to 5000ft amsl. The symbol before the D denotes that a Danger Area Activity Information Service is available for this area

A Danger Area Crossing Service (DACS) is available for certain danger areas. Contact frequencies are given are given on the Chart of United Kingdom Restrictions and Hazardous Areas, ENR 6-5-1-1, and in the legends of the 1:500,000 UK ICAO aeronautical charts.

A Danger Area Activity Information Service (DAAIS) is available for certain danger areas. The purpose of the service is to enable pilots to obtain an airborne update of the activity status of a Danger Area via a Nominated Service Unit, (NSU). To obtain information concerning the activity status of a danger area, pilots should call the appropriate NSU on the given frequency. If there is no reply from the NSU, pilots should assume that the danger area is active.

If an aircraft inadvertently enters an area notified as a restricted, prohibited or danger area, the commander must, unless otherwise instructed by radio by Air Traffic Control (ATC), or the airspace authority, leave the area as quickly as possible and not descend whilst over the area.

▶ Areas of Intensive Aerial Activity (AIAA)

There are several areas designated as AIAA. The geographic and vertical limits are shown on aeronautical charts and pilots are strongly recommended to avoid these areas of intense activity altogether. Pilots unable to avoid the areas should keep a good lookout and are strongly advised to make use of a radar service if available.

The line made of diamond shapes depicts the boundary of the Oxford Area of Intense Aerial Activity (AIAA) as depicted on a 1:500,000 aeronautical chart. The suggested radar service is Brize Radar, frequency 124.275

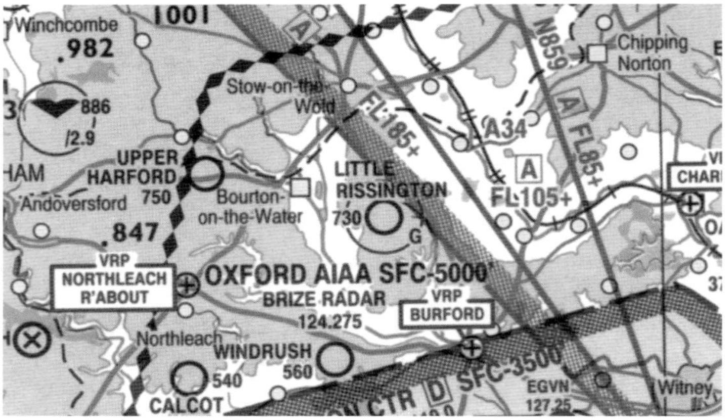

▶ Military Low Flying

Military low flying occurs over many parts of the UK at heights between 100ft and 2000ft above the surface. The greatest concentration is between 250 and 500ft above ground level and civil pilots are advised to avoid this height band whenever possible.

▶ Aerial Tactics Areas

Air combat training by military aircraft practising high energy manoeuvres regularly takes place in the areas listed in ENR 5-2-4. Pilots unable to avoid these areas are strongly advised to make use of a radar service.

▶ Military Training Areas (MTA) and Military Temporary Reserved Airspace (MTRA)

In the upper airspace, intense military flying training often takes place in Military Training Areas and Military Reserved Airspace. Details are at ENR 5-2-1.

▶ Small Arms Ranges

ENR 5-3-7/9 gives details of the small arms ranges notified to the authority which might pose a hazard to flight below 500ft above ground level (agl). The small arms ranges may be in use at any time and pilots are strongly advised to avoid these areas.

▶ High Intensity Radio Transmission Area (HIRTA)

Airspace of defined dimensions within which there is radio energy of such an intensity that it may cause interference with, and on rare occasions damage to, communications and navigation equipment.

HIRTA are marked on aeronautical charts with a name identification and activity upper limit as an altitude (based on the QNH altimeter setting)

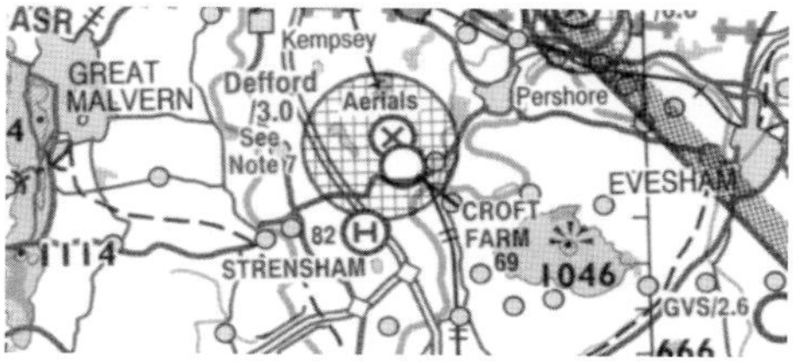

The Defford High Intensity Radio Transmission Area as depicted on a 1:500,000 aeronautical chart. This area is noted as effective to 3000ft amsl

▶ Bird Hazards

There are several areas in the UK where there is an intensity of bird movement activity. These are marked on the aeronautical charts with a name identification and activity upper limit as an altitude (based on QNH). Pilots should avoid flying through the areas if possible.

An area of intensive bird activity as depicted on a 1:500,000 aeronautical chart. This one is Otmoor and warns of activity up to 2000ft amsl

It has been shown that the risk of collision with birds is reduced when the aircraft is flown at slower speeds. If you encounter a flock of birds in flight try to reduce airspeed to less than 80 knots to reduce the risk of collision and extent of possible damage. If an aircraft suffers a bird strike it must be reported to the CAA.

▶ Hang Gliding, Paragliding and Parascending Sites

Sites where Hang Gliding, Paragliding and Parascending activities are known to take place are listed at ENR 5-5-2-1/3. Activity is weather dependant and pilots flying near these areas should be aware of the likelihood of activity.

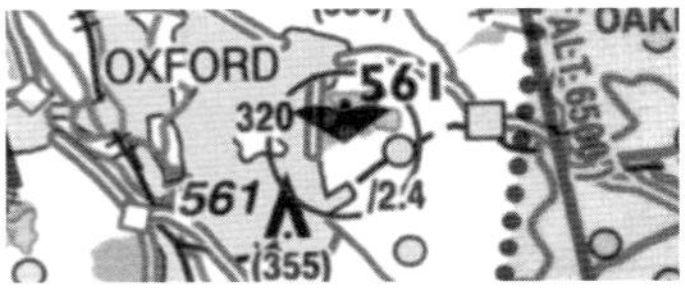

A hang gliding site as depicted on a 1:500,000 aeronautical chart. The circle warns of winch launching up to 2400ft amsl

▶ Glider Launching

Sites where glider launching is known to take place are listed at ENR 5-5-1-1/6. Activity is weather dependant and pilots flying near these areas should be aware of the likelihood of activity.

▶ Cable Launching Hang Gliders, Paragliders, Parascenders and Gliders

Winch launching by cable up to 2000ft Above Ground Level (agl) takes place at many activity sites. At some sites the limit is higher. Pilots should avoid crossing a launch site unless they have confirmed that winching is not taking place. Aeronautical charts show the altitude that cable launches can go to, in thousands of feet, at the side of the activity area boundary circle.

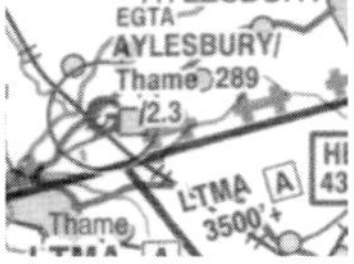

A glider launch site as depicted on a 1:500,000 aeronautical chart. This one is Aylesbury/Thame. The aerodrome level is 289ft amsl and winch launching may take place up to 2300ft amsl

▶ Microlight Flying

Microlight flying takes place at general activity airfields and specific locations. The locations may or may not be suitable for use by heavier aircraft.

A microlight flying site as depicted on a 1:500,000 aeronautical chart. This one is Oakley, the aerodrome elevation is 249ft amsl

▶ Balloon Launching

There are many captive and free manned balloon launch sites where balloon launching takes place. Some sites are more active than others and are shown and identified on aeronautical charts

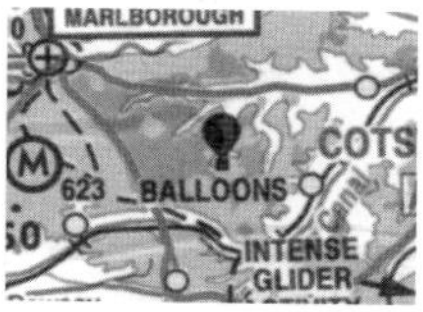

Balloon launch site as depicted on a 1:500,000 aeronautical chart

The Meteorological Office also conducts weather balloon ascents at certain centres and aerodromes.

▶ Gas Venting Operations

Severe turbulences and power fluctuations can be experienced over gas venting stations during the venting of natural (Methane) gas under high pressure. Locations of gas venting stations are listed at ENR 5-5-3/6 and shown on aeronautical charts with a name identification and activity upper limit as an altitude (based on the QNH altimeter setting).

Three Gas Venting Stations (GVS) as depicted on a 1:500,000 aeronautical chart. These warn of gas venting to 1100ft, 1300ft and 1200ft amsl

▶ Free-fall Parachuting

Free-fall parachuting takes place at sites listed at ENR 5-5-4-1/4. Parachuting may also take place at any Government or licensed aerodrome.

An airfield with parachuting activity as depicted on a 1:500,000 aeronautical chart. The drop zone has a radius of 1·5 nautical miles. The inner circle with a G at lower right at this particular site indicates that gliding is an additional activity

Parachuting can take place up to Flight Level 150 (approximately 15,000ft). Parachutists are required to operate only in conditions that enable them to remain clear of cloud with an in-flight visibility of at least 5 kilometres.

Pilots should avoid flying through parachute dropping areas unless they can confirm that no activity is taking place during the period of the crossing.

▶ En-route Obstacles

Obstacles which are 300 feet or more in height (above ground level) will be marked on the aeronautical navigation charts.

Obstacles should be lit if:

- They exceed 492 feet (150 metres) above ground level (agl).
- They are 492 feet in height or less, but, by virtue of their nature or location, are considered to present a significant hazard to air navigation.

A single, lit, obstruction as depicted on a 1:500,000 aeronautical chart. The top of this one is 996ft amsl and 556ft above ground level (agl)

A multiple, lit, obstruction as depicted on a 1:500,000 aeronautical chart. The top of this one, Didcot power station, is 850ft amsl and 656ft above ground level (agl)

▶ Flarestacks

Obstacles listed as 'Flarestacks' are those which burn off high pressure gas. The flame, which may not be visible in bright sunlight, can extend up to 600 feet.

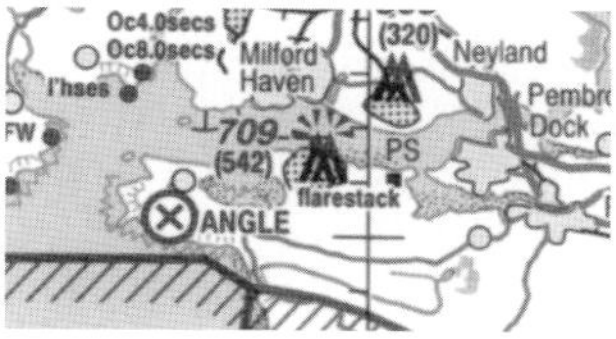

A flarestack as depicted on a 1:500,000 aeronautical chart. The top of this one is 709ft amsl and 542ft above ground level (agl)

▶ Hills and Mountains

Some hills and mountains which, by virtue of their height and position, are considered to be hazards to aviation are marked by red obstacle lights. The hills are shown on the aeronautical navigation charts.

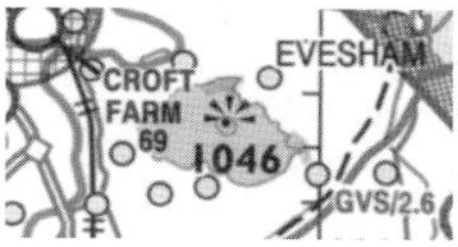

The five flashes show a hill with a warning light as depicted on a 1:500,000 aeronautical chart. The summit of this hill is 1046ft amsl, but it is situated in a valley region and so considered to be a hazard to navigation

▶ Revision

70 An area of airspace shown on an aeronautical chart with the annotation 'P203/2.4'

indicates:

A A danger area, number 203, active to 240 feet above ground level

B A prohibited area, number 203, active to 2400 feet above sea level

C A prohibited area active between 203 feet above ground level and 2400 feet above ground level

D Purple airspace, number 203, active to 2400 feet above sea level

71 A danger area marked on the chart with a broken outline is a:

A Scheduled danger area active at times notified by AIC

B Scheduled danger area with a standard published activity timetable

C Notified danger area active at times notified by NOTAM

D Notified danger area with a standard published activity timetable

72 If an aircraft inadvertently enters an active danger area the pilot should:

A Descend to minimum level and leave the area by the shortest route

B Maintain heading and height

C Maintain height and reverse the course to leave the area along the flight path that they have just flown

D Maintain height and leave the area by the shortest route

---

73 When flying in an Area of Intensive Aerial Activity (AIAA):

A The pilot must be in radio contact with a radar service

B The pilot is recommended to make use of a radar service

C The pilot must file a flight plan

D The aircraft must not be flown above 500 feet to avoid conflict with military traffic

---

74 The main concentration of low level military operation takes place:

A Between 100 and 250 feet above sea level

B Between 100 and 350 feet above ground level

C Between 500 and 1000 feet above ground level

D Between 250 and 500 feet above ground level

---

75 Small arms ranges are shown on the chart of Airspace Restrictions and Hazardous Areas. It is recommend that pilots do not fly within a certain distance of these. That distance is:

A 100 feet

B 500 feet

C 600 metres

D 1000 metres

---

76 Why is it recommended that pilots avoid flying within a High Intensity Radio or Radar Transmission Area?

A The transmissions may interfere with radio equipment carried in the aircraft

B The transmissions may interfere with the pressure instruments fitted to the aircraft

C The transmissions may damage the structure of the aircraft

D The transmissions may effect the accuracy of the chart

---

77 When flying in an area of intensive bird activity pilots are warned that:

A Flight at very low speeds confuses birds and there is a greater risk of collision

B Flight at very high speeds minimises the risk of a collision with a bird

C Flight at very low level reduces the risk of a collision with a bird

D Flight at speeds below 80 knots minimises the risk of a collision with a bird

---

78 If an aircraft suffers a bird strike:

A The incident must be reported to the CAA

B The incident must be reported to the RSPB

C The incident must be reported to the local Police

D The incident need not be reported but the aircraft must be inspected before further flight

79 To avoid the risk of collision with hang gliders and para gliders:

A Pilots should not fly upwind of hills

B Pilots should not fly lower than 500 feet above a hill

C Pilots should not fly downwind of hills

D Pilots should maintain a good lookout at all times

---

80 At any glider or hang glider winch launch site the cable can be expected to reach at least:

A 2500 feet above sea level

B 2500 feet above ground level

C 2000 feet above ground level

D 3000 feet above sea level

---

81 On an aeronautical chart the symbol 'GVS/3.5' indicates:

A A High Intensity Radio area to 3500 feet above ground level

B A High Intensity Radio area to 3500 feet above sea level

C A Gas Venting Station avoid up to 3500 feet above ground level

D A Gas Venting Station, avoid up to 3500 feet above mean sea level

---

82 The minimum visibility in which free fall parachuting may take place is:

A 1.5 kilometres

B 3 kilometres

C 5 kilometres

D 10 kilometres

---

83 Vertical obstructions such as masts or buildings must be notified to CAA, and will then be shown on aeronautical charts, if they reach a certain minimum height above ground level. That height is:

A 100 feet

B 300 feet

C 492 feet

D 999 feet

---

84 Although any obstruction may be lit, obstructions which reach a certain height above ground level must be lit. That height is

A 150 feet

B 300 feet

C 492 feet

D 999 feet

Answers on page 170

International Flights

International Flights

- Customs and Immigration Requirements
- The Prevention of Terrorism Act

▶ Customs and Immigration Requirements

When flying from the UK to a country that is a member state of the European Union (EU), there is no Customs restriction on the places of take-off for flights, nor is there any need for details of the flight to be notified to Customs. The first landing in any other EU state (unlike the UK) may have to be at a designated customs aerodrome you should check each countries requirements.

When returning to the UK from another EU state there is no Customs restriction on the places of landing. However, unless the aircraft is arriving at a designated Customs airport, the Customs and the Immigration department must be advised of the flight and passenger details with at least four hours notice of the intended arrival time at the first UK landing site to allow them to meet the aircraft if they choose to do so. Full details of procedures can be founding the GEN section of the AIP. Designated Customs Airports are listed in the AD section of the AIP and are shown on 1:500,000 aeronautical charts by a pecked line around the airport name.

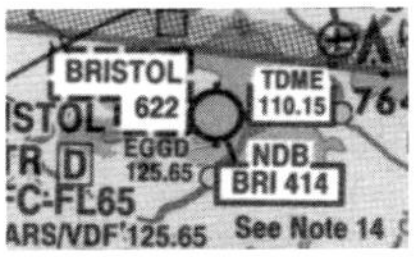

A customs airport as depicted on a 1:500,000 aeronautical chart

If an aircraft on an international flight is required to land at a place other than the declared destination Customs and Immigration should be informed as soon as possible and no person should leave the vicinity, unless in an emergency, without permission.

▶ The Prevention of Terrorism Act

The Prevention of Terrorism Act requires that aircraft operating between Great Britain and the Republic of Ireland, Northern Ireland, Isle of Man or the Channel Islands must arrive or depart via certain designated airports, unless prior police permission has been obtained.

Royal Flights

Royal Flights

- Royal Flights
- Royal Flights in Fixed-wing Aircraft
- Royal Flights in Helicopters
- Notification of Royal Flights
- Revision

▶ Royal Flights

A Royal Flight over the United Kingdom is a flight of a civil or military aircraft carrying one or more of the principal members of the Royal Family. Flights within the UK airspace by other members of the Royal Family, other reigning Sovereigns, prime Ministers and other Heads of State of the Commonwealth and foreign countries may also be offered Royal Flight status.

▶ Royal Flights in Fixed-wing Aircraft

Whenever possible, Royal Flights in fixed wing aircraft take place within the airways system and controlled airspace and are subject to normal ATC procedures. Where the route of a Royal Flight will take the aircraft outside controlled airspace, temporary controlled airspace (CAS-T) will be established.

Temporary control zones will be established around airfields of departure and destination where no permanent control zone exists. Control zones for Royal Flights will normally have a 10nm radius from the centre of the airfield and extend from ground level to a designated Flight Level. For outbound flights the control zone will be established for a period of 15 minutes before Estimated Time of Departure (ETD) until 30 minutes after ETD. For inbound flights the control zone is established for a period of 15 minutes before, until 30 minutes after, the ETA of the Royal aircraft at the airfield.

Temporary control areas will be established to meet the specific requirements of a Royal Flight. The lateral and vertical limits and the duration and the controlling authority of such areas will be promulgated via NOTAM.

Temporary controlled airways will be established to join temporary or permanent control zones or control areas, for 15 minutes before ETD at the departure airfield until 30 minutes after ETA at the destination. These airways will extend 5nm each side of the intended track of the Royal Flight and their vertical limits will be as designated.

A temporary control zone or area may be cancelled by the controlling authority when the Royal aircraft has left the zone or area and is established en-route, or has landed.

CAS-T will normally be notified as Class A airspace and also notified under Rule 21 of the Rules of the Air Regulations, meaning that Instrument Flight Rules (IFR) applies at all times. Gliders are not permitted to fly in CAS-T.

▶ Royal Flights in Helicopters

CAS-T is not normally established for Royal Flights in helicopters. For Royal helicopter flights a Royal Low Level Corridor (RLLC) marked by a series of check points. The check points will normally no more than 20 minutes flying time apart and coincide with turning points.

Pilots of military aircraft are prohibited from flying within certain distances of a RLLC. Civil pilots are not restricted in this way but are advised to keep a good lookout and maintain adequate separation from a Royal helicopter.

▶ Notification of Royal Flights

Information concerning a Royal Flight, giving full flight details including information on the establishment of CAS-T and vertical limits, is promulgated by NOTAM.

A freephone telephone service (on 0500 354802) gives a recorded message of daily information on Royal Flights and also includes details of Restricted Areas Temporary (RAT) such as those established for the RAF Red Arrows flying display team.

▶ Revision

85 Flights in fixed wing aircraft carrying a member of the Royal Family may be in part conducted outside existing airspace. For these portions of the flight:

A Temporary controlled airspace may be established

B The flight will not take place

C Class G airspace is established

D Class D airspace is established

Answers on page 170

Air Traffic Services

Air Traffic Services

- Flight Information Service (FIS)
- Air Traffic Control Service (ATC)
- Aerodrome Flight Information Service (AFIS)
- Aerodrome Air Ground Communications Service (A/G)
- BMAA Radio Frequency
- Revision

▶ Flight Information Service (FIS)

A Flight Information Service (FIS) is provided to all aircraft in FIR and UIR which are in contact with an Air Traffic Service Unit, (ATSU). This service includes information and warnings on meteorological conditions, changes of serviceability in navigational aids, condition of aerodrome facilities and other safety information.

▶ Air Traffic Control Service (ATC)

An Air Traffic Control (ATC) service is provided to aircraft in radio contact with an air traffic control unit. The service is available inside and outside controlled airspace and pilots are assumed to be complying with instructions unless they state otherwise.

At aerodromes outside controlled airspace the service offered can vary from an aerodrome control service only, to a full aerodrome, approach and approach radar service. The term 'air traffic control' is confined to those units which provide services by licensed controllers who are regulated by the CAA. All air traffic controllers provide flight information and alerting services in addition to air traffic control services. Other services available outside controlled airspace from an ATC unit include Radar Advisory Service and Radar Information Service.

A Radar Information Service (RIS) is offered to aircraft by ATC radar operators. RIS provides a service to the pilot warning of possible conflicting traffic. Under RIS the controller does not suggest avoiding action and the pilot is responsible for safe separation from the other traffic. The advantage of RIS is that the controller is acting as another pair of eyes, which helps the pilot greatly especially in congested airspace or when workload is high for other reasons.

Under RIS the pilot may be asked to maintain a particular height or heading to assist the operator. The pilot must tell ATC if they wish to alter height or heading. RIS can be requested for IFR or VFR flight inside or outside controlled airspace.

A Radar Advisory Service (RAS) can also be offered to aircraft by an ATC radar operator. RAS provides a service to the pilot warning of possible conflicting traffic and offering advice on avoiding action to be taken. If the pilot cannot take the action for any reason he or she should report that fact so that an alternative course of action can be offered by the controller.

When under RAS the pilot may be asked to maintain a particular height or heading to assist the controller. Pilots must tell ATC if they wish to alter height or heading as the change may bring the aircraft into conflict with other aircraft using the service.

RAS can be requested for IFR flights only, inside or outside controlled airspace.

It is especially important to appreciate the limitations of all radar services. Small, slow-moving aircraft such as balloons, microlights and gliders may not show up well on radar. Further, aircraft with little metal mass may also give poor radar returns. Even when receiving a radar service, pilots are advised to maintain a good lookout during flight and not rely on the radar controller solely for aircraft avoidance.

ATC callsign suffix's include 'Approach', 'Radar' and 'Tower' eg 'Brize Norton Radar'.

▶ Aerodrome Flight Information Service (AFIS)

An Aerodrome Flight Information Service (AFIS) is provided to aircraft at an aerodrome or in the vicinity of an aerodrome and consists of information relevant to assist in the safe conduct of flight. It may include traffic information and aerodrome activity and operating details. A typical service would provide details of runway in use, circuit direction and airfield altimeter pressure settings to pilots flying at, and in the vicinity of, the airfield.

An AFIS is provided by CAA-licensed operators called Flight Information Service Officers, (FISO). The FISO are not controllers and are not allowed to give permissions or clearances to aircraft in flight. However, FISO are permitted to give instructions to aircraft moving on the ground.

The callsign suffix for an AFIS is 'Information' eg 'Oxford Information'.

▶ Aerodrome Air Ground Communications Service (A/G)

Aerodromes which do not have ATC or AFIS may be allocated a frequency for use to allow the aerodrome operator to communicate with aircraft using the aerodrome. Radio operators are not permitted to imply in any way that they are providing an air traffic control or aerodrome flight information service.

The callsign suffix for an Aerodrome Air Ground Communications Service is 'Radio' eg Enstone Radio.

▶ BMAA Radio Frequency

The BMAA has been allocated a frequency for use by ground-based stations at microlight club airfields where no other frequency is in use. The frequency is 129.825MHz. This frequency is not for air-to-air use.

▶ Revision

86 When flying in Class G airspace a Flight Information Service may be provided by:

A A radar unit only

B An approach unit only

C An ATC or AFIS unit

D No radio service. Flight information service is only available in controlled airspace

87 An Air Ground Communications Service at an aerodrome, with the callsign suffix "Radio":

A May not control aircraft movements at any time

B May control aircraft movements on the ground but not in the air

C May control aircraft movements in the air and on the ground

D May control aircraft movements in the air but not on the ground

88 Aircraft flying under a Radar Information Service:

A Are controlled and provided with an information service on all other aircraft

B Are not controlled but are provided with a separation service from all other aircraft

C Are controlled and provided with a separation service from aircraft flying under IFR

D Are not controlled but are provided with an information service

Answers on page 170

Altimeter Setting Procedures

Altimeter Setting Procedures

- ▶ The Altimeter
- ▶ QNH
- ▶ Regional Pressure Setting
- ▶ QFE
- ▶ Standard Altimeter Setting
- ▶ Transition Altitude
- ▶ Transition Level
- ▶ Transition Layer
- ▶ Use of the Altimeter
- ▶ Quadrantal Rule
- ▶ Revision

▶The Altimeter

The altimeter enables a pilot to accurately establish the vertical position of the aircraft and so navigate in three dimensions. This allows the pilot to ensure safe vertical separation from other aircraft when under the control of an airspace controlling authority and also enables the pilot to keep clear of, or stay within, controlled airspace as depicted on aeronautical charts.

The altimeter reacts to changes in atmospheric pressure. It responds to reductions in pressure by displaying increasing altitude. Increases in pressure are displayed as reducing altitude.

Atmospheric pressure varies horizontally across the world as well as vertically through the atmosphere and the altimeter cannot distinguish between the two. The altimeter in an aircraft flown in level flight towards an area of lower pressure will react to the reduction in pressure by showing a climb. The pilot will try to maintain a steady altimeter reading by descending and so begin to fly lower than the altimeter actually indicates. The result may be to fly the aircraft dangerously low with the risk of colliding with high ground or obstructions.

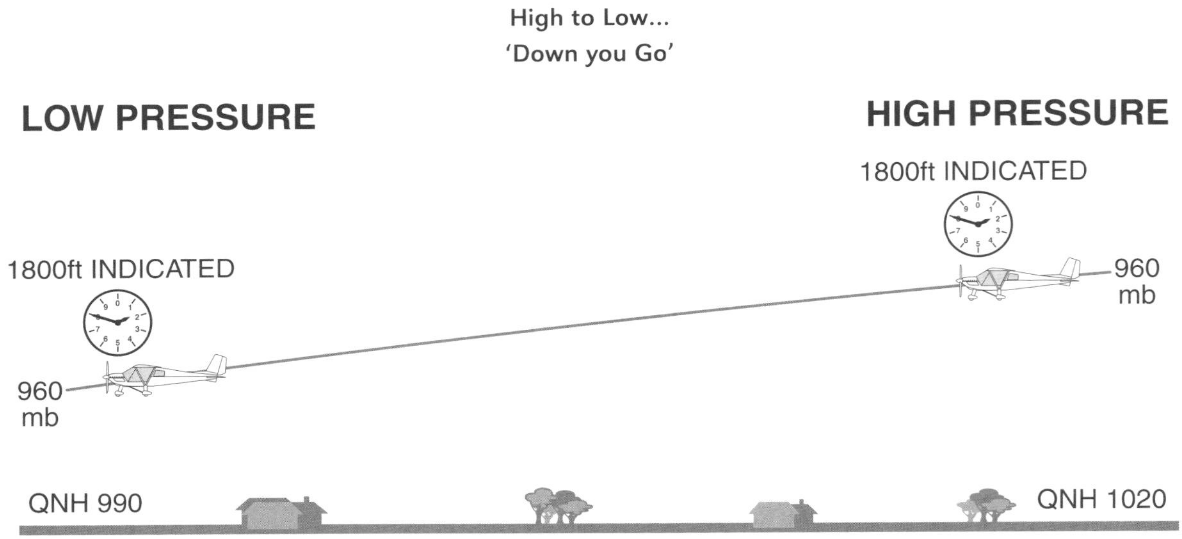

Flying from high pressure to low pressure, the aircraft will actually descend if following a constant pressure level

An Altimeter

Altimeters have the capacity to be re-set during flight so that they can continue to give an accurate indication of level, even though the atmospheric pressure in the region is changing. The altimeter re-setting is achieved by setting the required atmospheric pressure in view on a subscale on the altimeter face. The subscale setting is the pressure setting to which the altimeter is calibrated. When the actual atmospheric pressure on the altimeter is the same as that set on the subscale, the altimeter will read zero.

▶ QNH

QNH is the code to indicate an altimeter setting for mean sea level pressure eg QNH 1020mb. This means that the mean sea level atmospheric pressure is 1020 millibars.

This altimeter indicates an **altitude** 550 feet on a **QNH** pressure setting of 1020 millibars

'Altitude' is the vertical distance from mean sea level, indicated on an altimeter when QNH is set on the altimeter subscale.

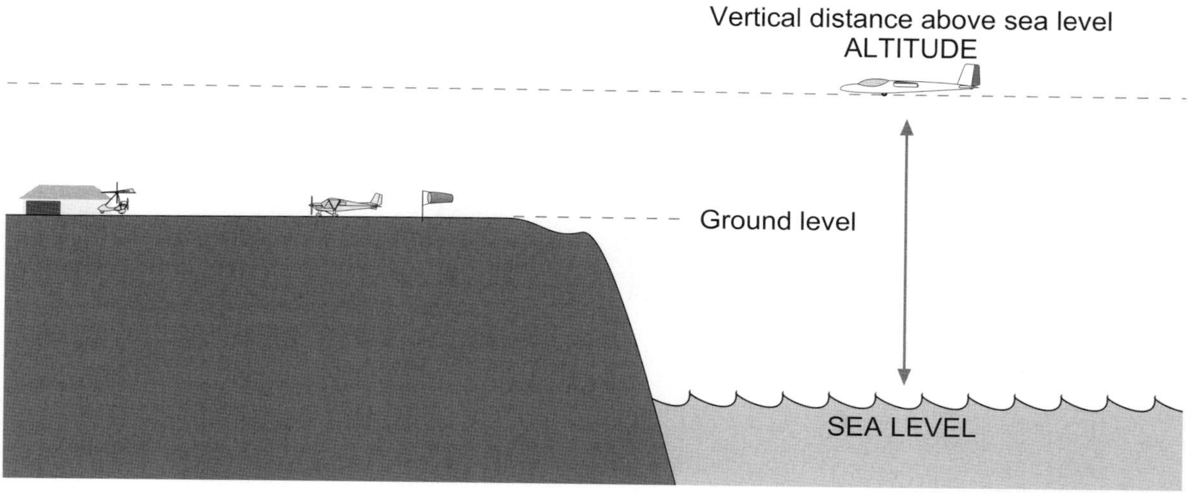

▶ Regional Pressure Setting

To ensure safe separation from other aircraft being controlled or coordinated by a controlling authority a pilot will be asked to set the same altimeter subscale setting as those other aircraft, by doing so all the aircraft altimeter readings will be coordinated with one another. Except within or below some specific types of controlled airspace, the setting passed to the pilot will be based on a geographic region and known as the Regional Pressure Setting or Regional QNH.

The Regional Pressure Setting is always given as the lowest forecast pressure within an Altimeter Setting Region, this means that whilst in that region the altimeter should never over-read the actual level and so the pilot will never be lower than the altitude indicated on the altimeter. This ensures adequate terrain and obstacle clearance.

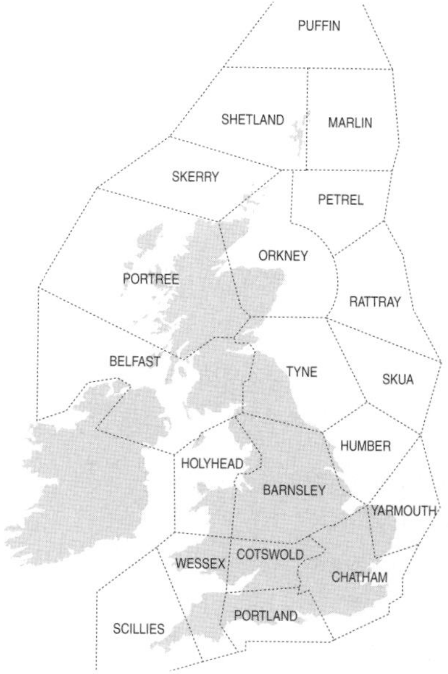

There are 20 Altimeter Setting Regions (ASR) in the UK. The ASR boundaries are shown on the navigation charts.

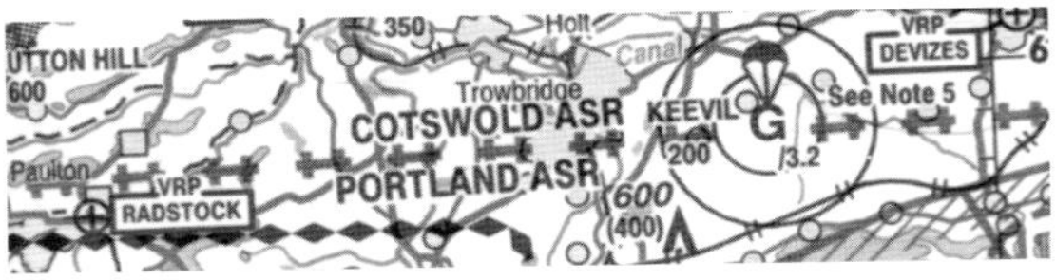

The boundary of two ASR as depicted on a 1:500,000 aeronautical chart

▶ QFE

QFE is the code to indicate an altimeter setting for airfield level pressure eg QFE 1000mb – the airfield atmospheric pressure is 1000 millibars.

This altimeter reads a **height** of zero feet when on the ground with the **QFE** setting of 1000 millibars

'Height' is the vertical distance from a specified place, indicated on an altimeter when QFE is set on the altimeter subscale.

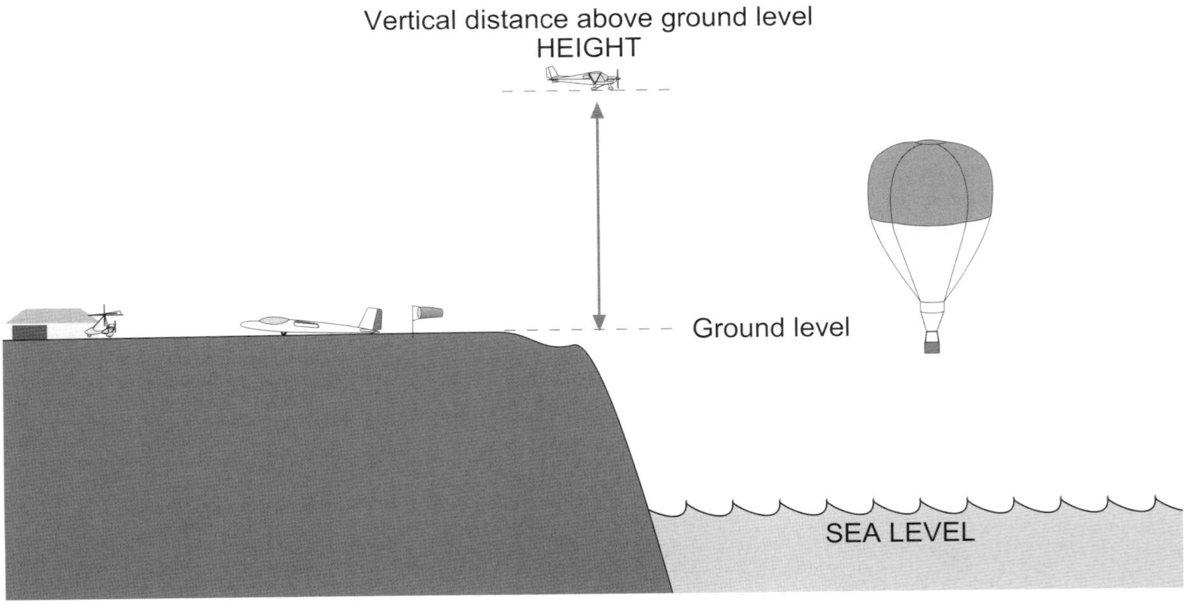

▶ Standard Altimeter Setting

To avoid the need to frequently update an altimeter subscale setting when flying on a long flight through changing pressure regions, and at relatively high levels where ground avoidance is not a factor but coordination with other aircraft is, a universal standard pressure setting of 1013.2 millibars can be used.

As the standard setting is not the actual QNH, the reading when 1013 is set on the altimeter is not an altitude but is instead referred to as a Flight Level (FL).

A 'Flight Level (FL)' is one of a series of levels of equal atmospheric pressure indicated in hundreds of feet on an altimeter set to the Standard Altimeter Setting of 1013.2mb. For example FL40 is shown on an altimeter as 4000 feet. It is usual in the UK to fly at Flight Levels separated by 500 feet intervals.

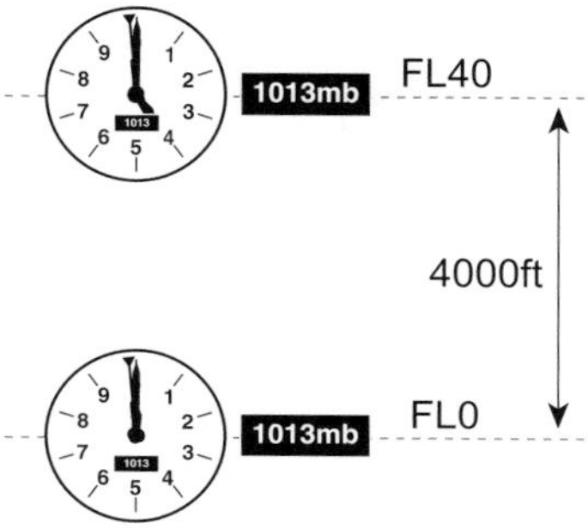

If the actual QNH of an area is lower than 1013.2 millibars, an altimeter set to 1013 will "zero" below sea level and the flight level indicated will be below the actual altitude (that is, less than the actual distance above mean sea level). For example if the QNH is 1003 millibars, an altimeter set to 1013.2 will indicate approximately 300 feet (FL3) when actually at sea level (because 1mb equals approximately 30ft and 10mb x 30ft = 300ft). Likewise the altimeter will read Flight Level 33 (FL33) when at in fact at 3000 feet altitude. When FL30 is shown on the altimeter the aircraft is 2700 feet above mean sea level (altitude).

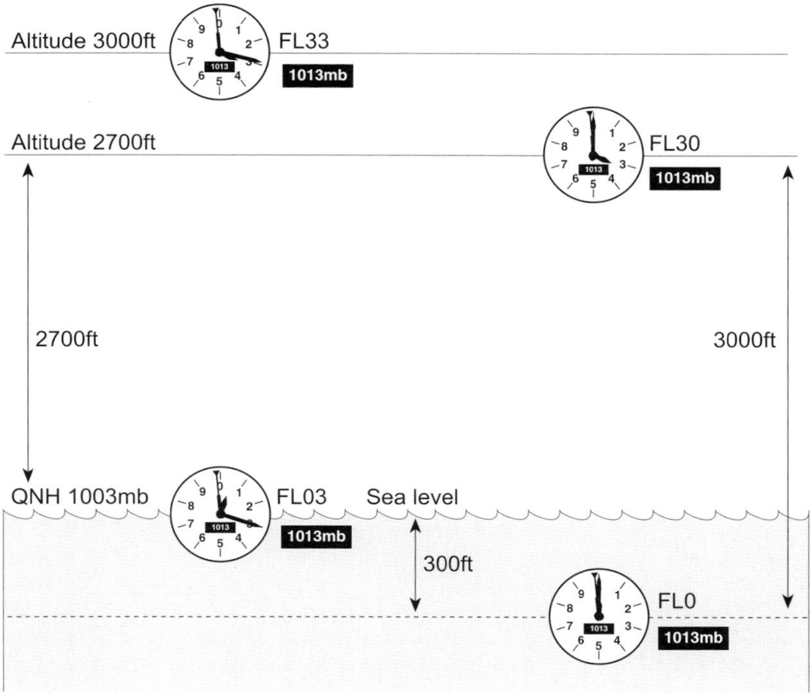

Conversely if the actual QNH is higher than 1013.2 the altimeter will "zero" above sea level and the flight level indicated will be above the equivalent altitude.

For example if the QNH is 1023 millibars an altimeter set to 1013.2 will show approximately minus 300 feet when the aircraft is actually at sea level and 2700 feet when the aircraft is at 3000 feet. When indicting FL30 the altimeter will actually be at 3300 feet above mean sea level.

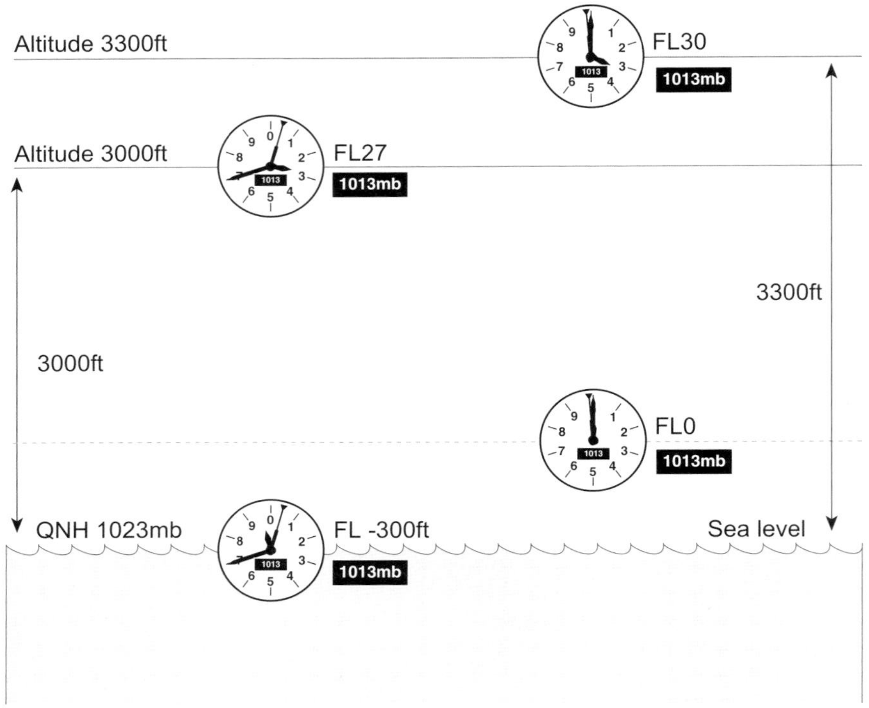

The average range of sea level pressure across the world is between 960 millibars and 1050 millibars giving a possible variation of actual Flight Level position of 2700 feet, based on 30 feet per millibar.

Because flight levels are not altitudes they cannot be used for ground or obstacle avoidance. The standard altimeter setting is not used below an altitude known as the Transition Altitude

▶Transition Altitude

Transition Altitude is the altitude at or below which the vertical position of the aircraft is controlled by reference to altitude. The general value of the transition altitude outside controlled airspace in the UK is 3000 feet. There are some exceptions specified in the ENR 1-7-1/4 section of the AIP. These exceptions principally apply to airspace within, or below, certain control zones and control areas.

▶Transition Level

Transition level is the lowest flight level available above the transition altitude. The actual level depends upon Transition Altitude and the actual QNH and so is not a standard figure. For example, if the Transition Altitude is 3000 feet and the QNH 1003, the Transition Level would be FL35 at 3200 feet. FL30 would be 2700 feet altitude, so it is below the Transition Altitude at and therefore not available.

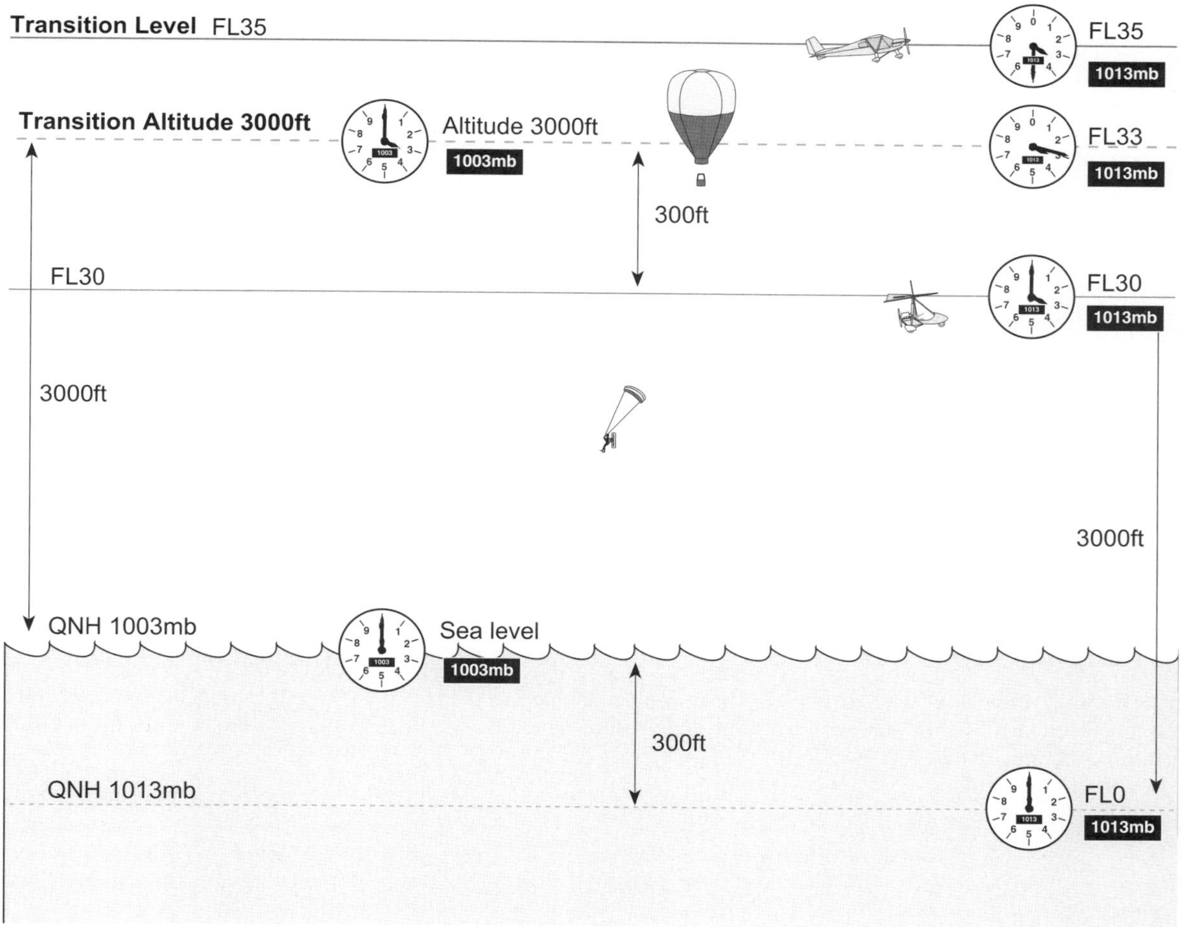

If the Transition Altitude was 3000 feet and the QNH 1023 the Transition Level would be FL30 which with this QNH is at 3300 feet altitude.

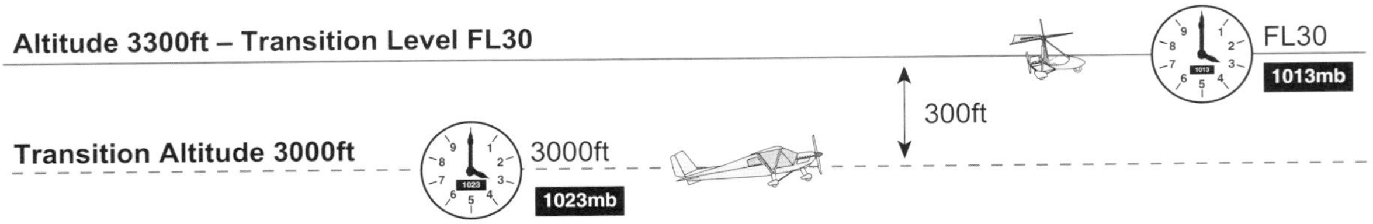

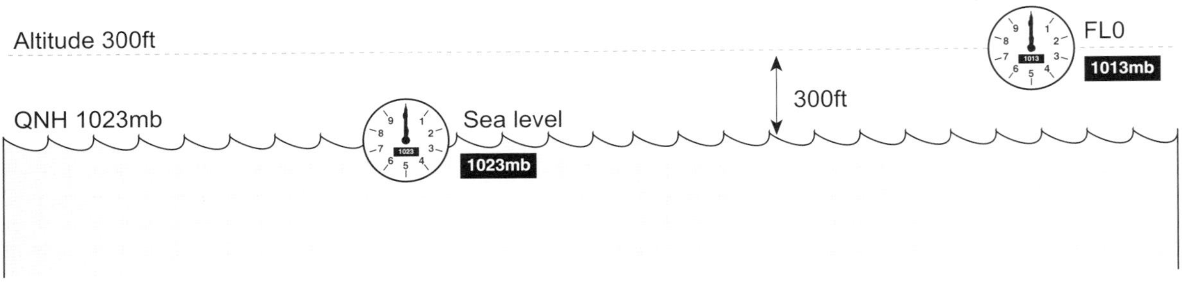

▶Transition Layer

The transition layer is the airspace between the transition altitude and the transition level. It is usual that there will be a layer between the transition altitude and transition layer although it will never be more than 500 feet (because Flight Levels are generally allocated in 500ft steps).

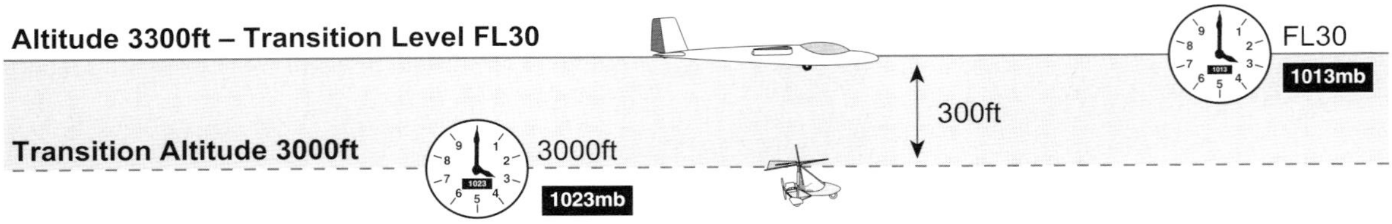

▶Use of the Altimeter

In the UK it is still usual for aircraft flying within the airfield circuit to set QFE so that the altimeter is indicating the height of the aircraft above the airfield. An aircraft approaching an airfield will call by radio to establish the QFE and then set that figure so that the join is made accurately either into the circuit or to join overhead.

The designated altimeter pressure setting point on an aerodrome is an area called the apron. The apron is an area set aside for parking, loading and unloading aircraft and is not part of the manoeuvring area which comprises of the taxiways and runways.

Away from the airfield an aircraft will usually set QNH in order that the altimeter reading is related to sea level and so the altimeter reading can be directly related to the surface elevations and airspace shown as altitudes on navigation charts.

When flying in contact with an air traffic service an aircraft may set Regional QNH (Regional Pressure Setting) as requested by the traffic service so that the altimeter indicated level is coordinated with all other aircraft using the same service on the same setting.

Aircraft flying below controlled airspace with a base level given as an altitude should set the QNH of the airfield controlling the airspace and not fly on a QFE or Regional Pressure Setting, this ensures that the aircraft will not stray into the controlled airspace as long as the altimeter reading is less than the lower level of the airspace as shown on the chart.

Aircraft flying above the transition altitude in controlled airspace may be asked by the controller to set the standard altimeter setting of 1013.2mb and fly at a particular Flight Level.

Aircraft flying VFR below airspace whose base is defined as a Flight Level should set the standard altimeter setting to ensure that they remain clear of the airspace. Because the Flight Level is related to the standard pressure and not the actual or regional QNH the flight level may be up to 1600 feet below or 1200 feet above the equivalent altitude. As a quick reference, if the QNH is lower than 1013 the flight level will be lower than the equivalent altitude. If the QNH is higher than 1013 the Flight Level will be higher than the equivalent altitude eg if the QNH is 993mb, FL45 is at 4200ft amsl. If the QNH is 1023mb, FL45 is at 4800ft amsl.

▶Quadrantal Rule

Instrument Flight Rule (IFR) traffic cruising outside controlled airspace below FL245 must do so in accordance with a procedure called the Quadrantal Rule. The Quadrantal Rule determines that aircraft cruising above the transition altitude select specified Flight levels depending upon the track direction that they fly. The track is measured to magnetic North and so variation is added or subtracted as appropriate to the drawn true track. The result is a magnetic track.

- Aircraft flying on a magnetic track of less than 090 will select an odd flight level in thousands of feet eg FL 30
- Aircraft flying on a magnetic track of 090-179 will select an odd flight level in thousands of feet plus 500ft eg FL 35
- Aircraft flying on a magnetic track of 180-269 will select an even flight level in thousands of feet eg FL 40.
- Aircraft flying on a magnetic track of 270 – 360 will select an even flight level in thousands of feet plus 500ft eg FL 45

Although the quadrantal rule only applies to IFR flights it is good practice for VFR flights to comply with it when cruising at levels above the transition altitude (usually 3000 feet amsl outside controlled airspace).

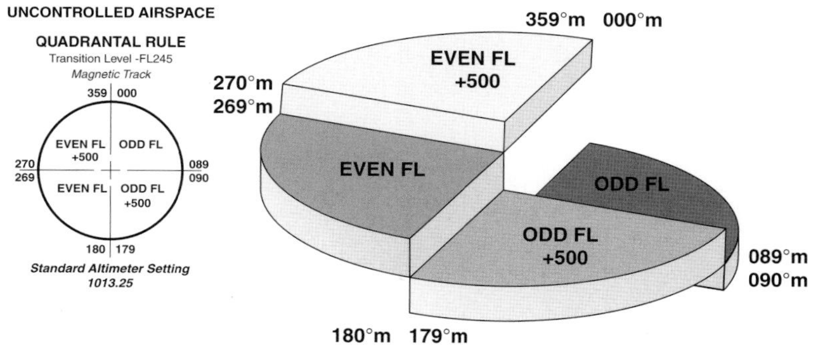

▶ Revision

89 An altimeter set reading zero at sea level is set to:

A QNH and reads altitude

B QFE and reads elevation

C Regional QNH and reads Flight Levels

D QNE and reads height

90 An aircraft flying below a Terminal Control Area (TMA) should set the altimeter to:

A Regional QNH

B The Standard Altimeter Setting

C The QFE of an aerodrome under the Terminal Manoeuvring Area

D The QNH of an aerodrome under the Terminal Control Area

91 The transition layer is:

A The layer between the surface and the transition level

B The layer between the transition altitude and the transition level

C The layer between the transition altitude and the ground

D The layer above the transition level

92 It is important to understand that Flight Levels are not always at the same position as their equivalent altitude. On a day when the QNH is 1023 millibars the actual altitude of Flight Level 50 will be approximately:

A 3000 feet

B 4700 feet

C 5000 feet

D 5300 feet

93 Although mandatory for IFR flight only, it is useful to understand the Quadrantal rule. An aircraft cruising on a magnetic track of 192 degrees would select a flight level which was:

A Odd numbered eg FL50

B Odd numbered plus 500 feet eg FL55

C Even numbered eg FL60

D Even numbered plus 500 feet eg FL65

Answers on page 170

Operational Procedures and Rules of the Air

Operational Procedures and Rules of the Air

- Authority of the Commander of an Aircraft
- Endangering Safety
- Drunkenness in Aircraft
- Pre-flight Actions
- Weather Reports and Forecasts
- Wake Turbulence
- Aviation Fuel
- Documents to be Carried
- Production of Documents
- Offences Relating to Documents
- Flight Plans
- Application of the Rules
- Reporting Hazardous Conditions
- Notification of Arrival and Departure
- Movement of Aircraft on Aerodromes
- Access to Aerodromes
- Right of Way on the Ground
- Right of Way During Take-off and Landing
- Order of Landing
- Flight in the Vicinity of an Aerodrome
- Revision

▶ Authority of the Commander of an Aircraft

Everyone on board an aircraft must obey all lawful orders which the aircraft commander gives for the safety of the aircraft and of people or property carried, or for the safety, efficiency or regularity of air navigation.

▶ Endangering Safety

A person must not recklessly or negligently act in a manner likely to endanger an aircraft or anyone in it, or cause or permit an aircraft to endanger anyone or any property.

▶ Drunkenness in Aircraft

A person must not board any aircraft when drunk, or be drunk in it. This includes passengers. A person must not, when acting as a crew member or being carried for the purpose, be under the influence of drink or a drug to such an extent as to impair his or her capacity so to act. Limits imposed in 2004 dictate that when acting as a pilot the blood alcohol level must not exceed 20 milligrams in 100 millilitres.

It is sensible to leave **at least** eight hours between drinking any amount of alcohol and flying.

▶ Pre-flight Actions

The pilot in command must reasonably satisfy himself before each flight that:

- the flight can be safely made, taking into account the latest information available as to route and aerodromes to be used, weather reports and forecasts available, and options open if the flight cannot be completed as planned;
- equipment required to be carried is carried and serviceable;
- the aircraft is fit for flight and that all required pre-flight checks have been carried out;
- any load carried is safe in terms of weight, distribution and security;
- enough fuel, oil and coolant is carried including a margin for safety;
- with regard to its performance the aircraft is capable of safely taking-off, reaching and maintaining a safe height and making a safe landing at the intended destination.

The pilot in command must also brief all passengers before the flight. The briefing must include:

- Details of use of any seat mechanism.
- Details of use of seat belts and safety equipment.
- Use of doors if applicable.
- What to do in the event of a forced landing or ditching.

▶ Weather Reports and Forecasts

Before flight an aircraft commander must study the appropriate reports and forecasts for the route and determine whether Instrument Meteorological Conditions (IMC) are likely to prevail at any point. Instrument Metrological Conditions means weather below VMC minima, in other words weather which does not permit flight in compliance with Visual Flight Rules.

Weather reports and forecasts are available from several sources. The Meteorological Office provide Terminal Aerodrome Forecasts (TAF), Meteorological Aerodrome Reports (METAR), surface pressure analysis and forecast charts, area forecast charts, spot wind reports and general weather forecasts. The reports and forecasts are available by telephone, fax back and internet.

Specific route forecasts can be made available with sufficient notice, at least 2 hours for flights less than 500 nautical miles.

Specialised forecasts can be obtained for recreational flying activities such as microlight flying, gliding, ballooning and hang gliding. These can be made available for specific sites up to twice daily.

An aircraft which is unable to communicate by radio with an air traffic control unit at the aerodrome of destination shall not begin flight to an aerodrome within a control zone if the information (which it is a reasonably practicable for the pilot of the aircraft to obtain) indicates that it will arrive at that aerodrome when the ground visibility is less than 10km or the cloud ceiling is less than 1500ft.

▶ Wake Turbulence

All aircraft produce turbulent air behind their flight and taxiing path. Some of the turbulence results from the movement of the aircraft propeller and the backwash it produces. The higher the power setting the more disturbed the air will be behind the propeller. As the pilot of a small aircraft you should be aware of the disturbance and avoid taxiing or flying close to another propeller-driven aircraft to avoid the effect of the backwash.

The aircraft shape also produces turbulence as it moves through the air in flight. The most pronounced disturbance comes as a result of the wingtip vortices generated as a result of high pressure span-wise airflow underneath the wing of the aircraft. The tip vortex is produced from the time of lift off until the time of touchdown and is most severe at high angles of attack and high wing loadings. Flying into the vortex produced by another aircraft can lead to loss of control and has resulted in serious, and even fatal, accidents.

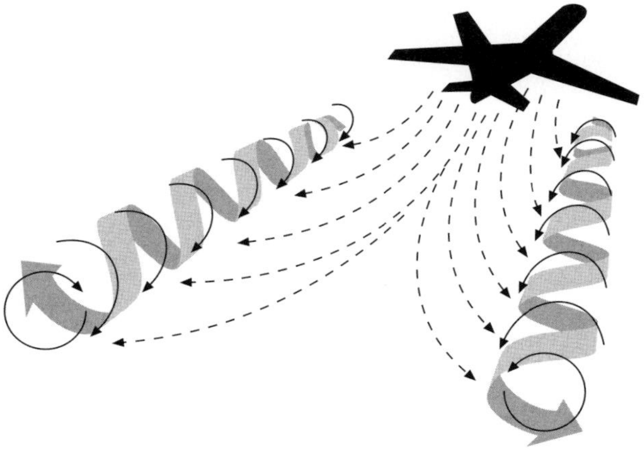

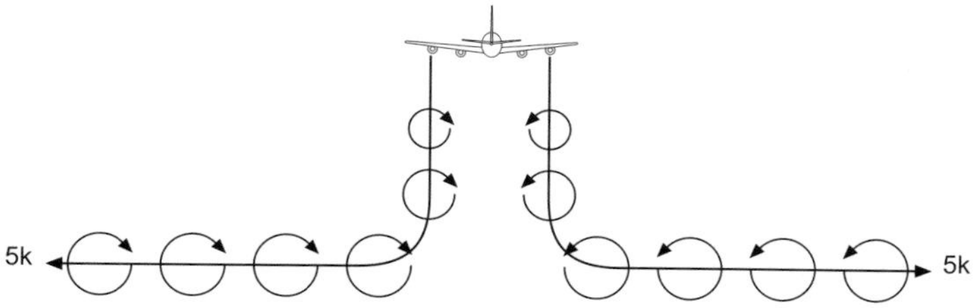

The tip vortex moves outward from the point of leaving the wing at an airspeed of about 5 knots

When taking-off or landing in still air conditions the vortices will move away from the flight path of the aircraft, clearing the runway line. If there is a crosswind the upwind vortex will be pushed back to the runway and the downwind vortex pushed faster away from the runway. In flight the vortex will also move outward from the aircraft flight path and tend to descend in stable air conditions, although it may climb in unstable air conditions.

When intending to fly behind another aircraft of any size the pilot should ensure that they will keep clear of the wake vortex of the other aircraft. The diagrams below show the likely position of the vortex produced in various phases of flight and the effects of crosswinds on the vortices.

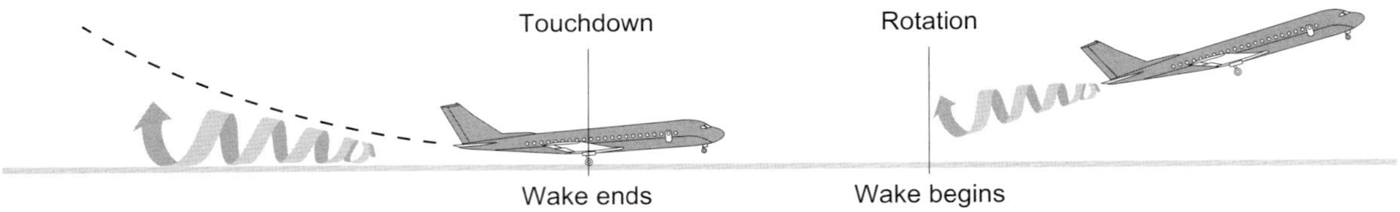

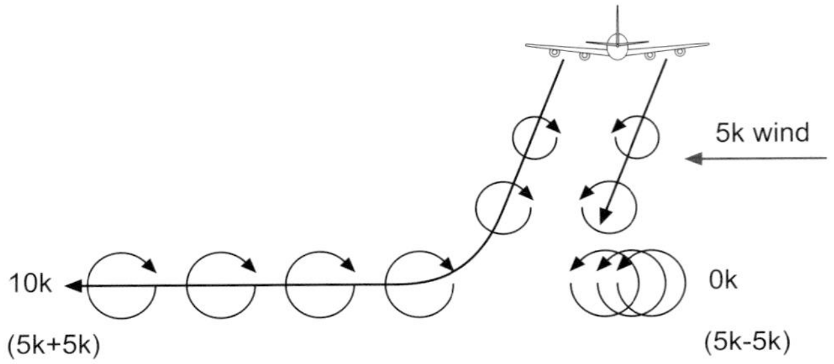

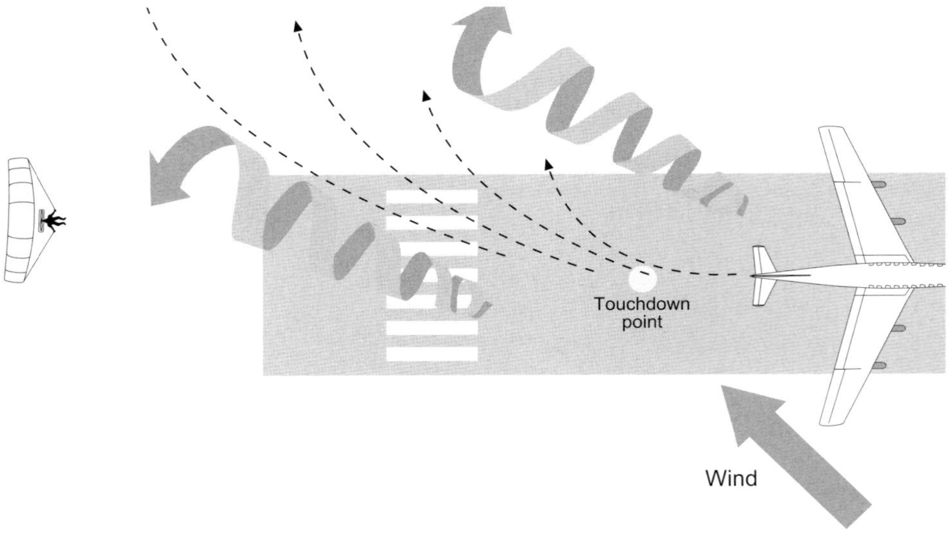

Separation times and distances between aircraft on approach to, and departing from, an airfield are set out. These times/distances depend upon the weight of the leading and following aircraft. The weight parameters are shown below in kilograms, you will see that there are differences between ICAO and UK definitions.

Category	ICAO and Flight Plan	UK
Heavy (H)	136,000 or greater	136,000 or greater
Medium (M)	7,000 – 136,000	40,000 – 136,000
Small (S) (UK only)	N/A	17,000 – 40,000
Light (L)	7,000 or less	17,000 or less

Wake Turbulence Spacing Minima – Final Approach

Leading Aircraft	Following Aircraft	Spacing distance Minima (nm) ICAO	UK
Heavy	Light	6	8
Medium	Light	5	6
Small	Light	3	4
Light	Light	–	None

Wake Turbulence Spacing Minima – Departures

Leading Aircraft	Following Aircraft	Minimum spacing at the time aircraft are airborne	
Heavy Medium Small	Light Light Light	Departing from the same position	2 minutes
Heavy Medium Small	Light Light Light	Departing from an intermediate point on the same runway	3 minutes

More detail can be found in an AIC, currently 17/1999 (Pink 188).

▶ Aviation Fuel

No person shall allow any fuel to be used in an aircraft if he or she knows or has reason to believe that it is not fit for such use. There are specific requirements for storing and sampling aviation fuel stocks at aerodromes, these are dealt with in the CAA publication CAP 748.

Fuel pumps and aircraft fuel tank caps are usually coloured to indicate the type of fuel supplied or used as the case may be. AVGAS (aviation petrol) filler points will be coloured red, AVTUR (jet A-1) aircraft filler points are coloured black. The use of motor fuel (MOGAS) requires certain details to be entered into the aircraft logbook to say that the aircraft may use that fuel. Details are available from the BMAA technical department.

▶ Documents to be Carried

The only private flights that require the pilot to carry documents in the aircraft are those which cross an international boundary. The UK airspace is divided into two basic areas called Flight Information Regions (FIR).

If a flight is planned to cross an outer boundary of either of the FIR (but not the boundary between them) the following documents must be carried:

- The radio licence.
- The licences of the members of the flight crew.
- The certificate of registration of the aircraft.
- A copy of the procedures to be followed when an aircraft is intercepted. A copy of these procedures is available as a PDF file to print off from the AIS web site (www.ais.org.uk).
- It is advisable to carry:
- The Permit to Fly. Although it is not valid outside the UK it may be accepted as proof of airworthiness in countries you visit, so it is worth taking with you.

▶ Production of Documents

The following documents must be produced at the request of an authorised person (i.e. any police constable, or anyone authorised by the Secretary of State or the CAA in a manner appropriate to the case):

- Aircraft Certificate of Registration.
- Permit to Fly and Certificate of Validity.
- Flight crew licences.
- Personal flying logbooks for up to two years after the last entry in any book.
- Licence for the aircraft radio.
- Interception procedures.

▶ Offences Relating to Documents

It is an offence to:

- Use a forged, altered, revoked or suspended document issued under the ANO, or to use one to which you are not entitled.
- Lend a document issued under the ANO, or otherwise allow it to be used by anyone else, with intent to deceive.
- Forge or render illegible any logbook or record required by the ANO, or to make a false or material omission, or to destroy it during the period for which it is required to be presented (all entries in such documents must be indelible).

▶ Flight Plans

Flight plans fall into two categories.

Full flight plans; the information required on Form CA 48.

Abbreviated flight plans; the limited information required to obtain a clearance for a portion of a flight, for example flying in a control zone, filed either by radio or telephone prior to take-off.

The full flight plan is an Air Traffic Service (ATS) message compiled on behalf of the pilot in command to a set format on Form CA 48, and then transmitted by the appropriate ATC authority to organisations concerned with the flight. The flight plan is the basis on which ATC clearance is given for the flight to proceed.

The destination aerodrome will be advised of the flight only if the flight plan information covers the whole route of the flight.

Completing the form correctly is important as many are processed by automatic systems. Full instructions are given in the UK AIP at ENR 1-10-1/2, with AIC updates.

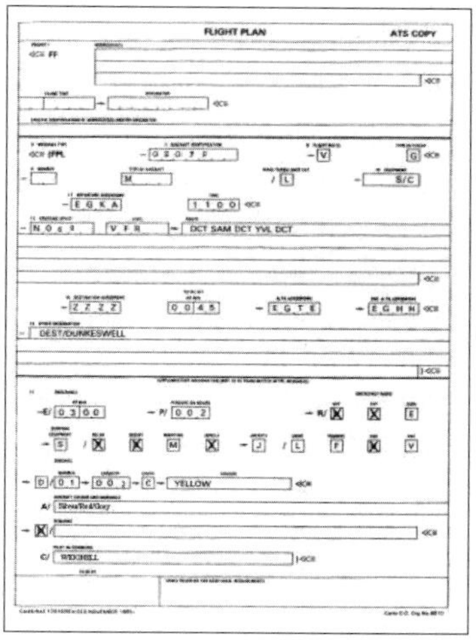

Normally flight plans should be filed on the ground with the ATS unit at the aerodrome of departure, at least 60 minutes before clearance to start up or taxy is requested. Exceptionally, in cases where it is impossible to meet this requirement, as much notice as possible should be given, never less than 30 minutes.

An airborne flight plan may be filed provided that the pilot leaves sufficient time for the clearance to be issued before the aircraft reaches the boundary of the controlled airspace (normally not less than 10 minutes).

- A pilot **may** file a flight plan for any flight.
- Pilots **must** file a flight plan:

For all flights in Class A, B, C and D airspace

When the pilot wishes to receive an air traffic advisory service (Class F airspace)

For all flights which will cross a UK international FIR boundary.

- A pilot is **advised** to file a flight plan:

If the flight involves flying over the sea more than 10 nautical miles from the coast or flying over sparsely populated areas where search and rescue operations would be difficult.

If it is intended to fly into an area where search and rescue operations are in progress. The flight plan should include the expected times of entering and leaving the area and the details must be passed to the parent Area Control Centre (ACC). The ACC will notify the Aeronautical Rescue Control Centre (ARCC) concerned.

If a pilot who has filed a flight plan lands at an aerodrome other than the destination specified, the air traffic service unit (ATSU) at the specified destination must be told within 30 minutes of the estimated time of arrival there.

▶Application of the Rules

The Rules of the Air apply to all the aircraft within the United Kingdom and all UK-registered aircraft wherever they may be. The rules may be departed from to the extent necessary to avoid immediate danger or for complying with the law of any country in which the aircraft might be. When a rule is departed from for safety reasons the circumstances must be reported afterwards to the competent authority (eg the CAA).

▶Reporting Hazardous Conditions

The commander of an aircraft must report to air traffic control any hazardous flight conditions encountered, as soon as possible, giving details pertinent to the safety of other aircraft.

▶Notification of Arrival and Departure

If an aircraft is expected at an aerodrome the commander must inform the authorities at the aerodrome as soon as possible if the destination is changed or if arrival will be delayed by 45 minutes or more. This is to avoid any unnecessary 'overdue action' being taken by the aerodrome.

Wherever possible an aircraft's commander must report to the appropriate authority at an aerodrome upon arrival, and prior to departure.

▶Movement of Aircraft on Aerodromes

An aircraft must not taxi on the apron or the manoeuvring area of an aerodrome without permission of the air traffic control unit or, in its absence, the aerodrome authority.

▶Access to Aerodromes

Except where there is a public right of way, a person or vehicle must not go on to any part of an aerodrome without permission of the person in charge of the aerodrome, and then act in accordance with any conditions given.

A vehicle or person must not go or move on the manoeuvring area of an aerodrome having an air traffic control unit except with the permission of that unit and only in accordance with any conditions.

▶Right of Way on the Ground

Regardless of any air traffic control clearance it is the duty of an aircraft commander to do everything possible to avoid collision with other aircraft or vehicles.

- Flying machines and vehicles must give way to aircraft landing or taking-off.
- Vehicles, and flying machines which are not taking-off or landing, must give way to any vehicle towing an aircraft.
- Vehicles which are not towing aircraft must give way to aircraft.

When two flying machines are approaching head-on, or nearly so, each must turn right.

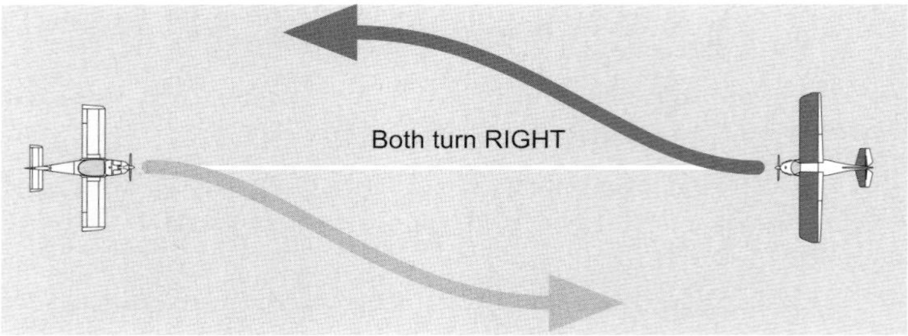

When two flying machines are converging on the ground the one which has the other on its right must give way, avoiding crossing ahead of the other unless passing well clear.

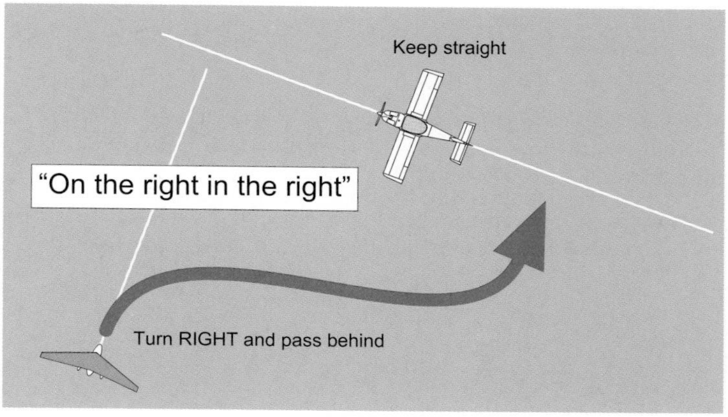

A flying machine which is being overtaken by another on the ground has right of way and the overtaking aircraft must keep out of the way by turning left until well clear.

Vehicles obey the normal UK rules of the road when overtaking or approaching another vehicle head-on.

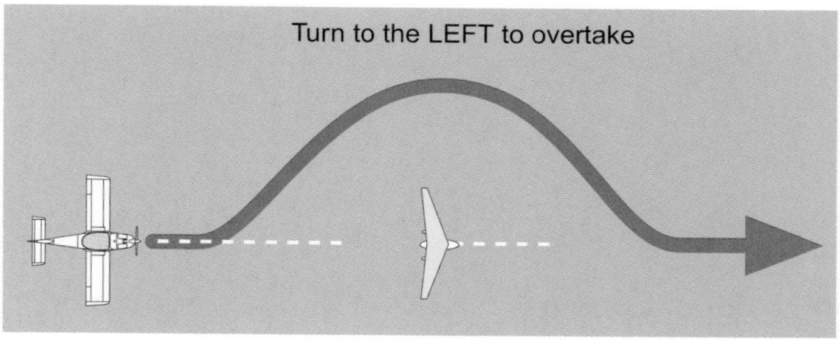

▶ Right of Way During Take-off and Landing

A flying machine, glider or airship must take-off and land in the direction indicated by ground signals or, in their absence, into wind unless good aviation practice demands otherwise.

A flying machine or glider must not land on a runway which is not clear of other aircraft unless an aerodrome air traffic control unit authorises otherwise.

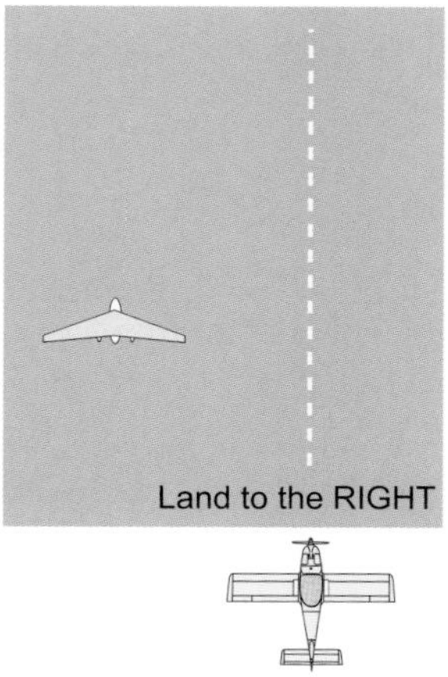

Where take-offs and landings are not confined to a runway, a landing flying machine or glider must leave clear on its left any aircraft which has landed or is already landing or about to take-off.

If such a flying machine or glider is about to turn, it must turn to the left only after the commander has satisfied himself that such action will not interfere with other traffic movements.

When take-offs and landings are not confined to a runway, a flying machine about to take-off must manoeuvre so as to leave clear on its left any aircraft which has already taken-off or is about to take-off.

After landing a flying machine must move clear of the landing area as soon as possible unless the aerodrome air traffic control unit authorises otherwise.

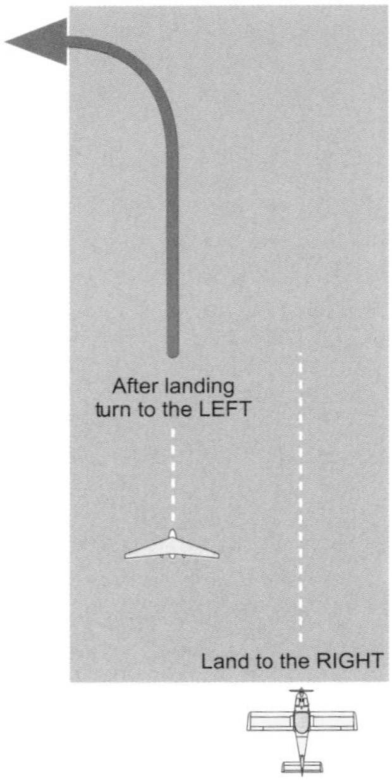

▶ Order of Landing

An aircraft landing or on the final approach to land has right of way over others in flight or on the surface

In the case of two or more flying machines, gliders or airships approaching any place for landing, the lower aircraft has right of way (although the lower aircraft must not cut in front of, or overtake another which on final approach).

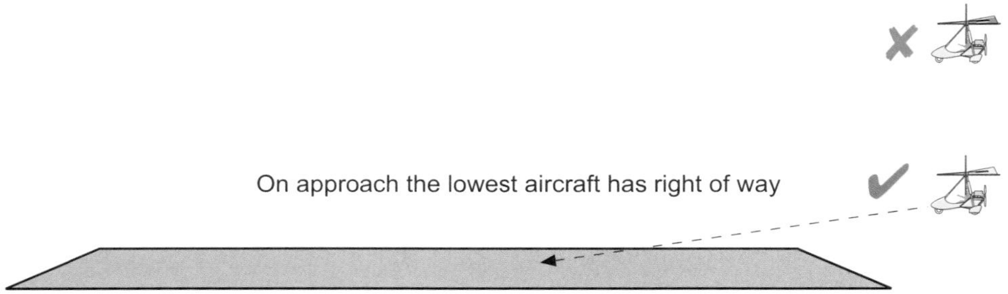

When air traffic control has given aircraft an order of priority for landing they must approach to land in that order. When the commander of an aircraft is aware that another is making an emergency landing, he or she must give way.

▶ Flight in the Vicinity of an Aerodrome

Subject to Rule 39 of the rules of the Air (which deals with flight in an Aerodrome Traffic Zone), a flying machine, glider or airship flying in the vicinity of an aerodrome or moving on an aerodrome shall, unless the aerodrome ATC unit authorises otherwise:

- conform to the traffic pattern formed by other aircraft intending to land at that aerodrome, or keep clear of the airspace in which the pattern is formed;
- make all turns to the left unless ground signals indicate otherwise.

▶ Revision

94 All persons shall obey the commander of an aircraft:

A At all times for any reason

B At all times if for the safety of the aircraft

C Only in the air

D Only on the ground

95 The legal limit for alcohol in the blood when piloting an aircraft is:

A 20 milligrams in 100 millilitres

B 40 milligrams in 100 millilitres

C 60 milligrams in 100 millilitres

D 80 milligrams in 100 millilitres

96 The responsibility for aircraft's preparation prior to flight is that of:

A The owner(s)

B The commander

C Air traffic control

D Jointly the commander and the owner

97 A pilot must brief the passengers before flight on items including:

A The length of time that the flight will take

B The route that the flight will take

C The use of the aircraft radio

D Actions to be taken in the event of an emergency

98 When taking-off from a runway shortly after another larger aircraft has departed, to avoid wake turbulence it is best to:

A Lift-off before the point at which the other aircraft lifted-off

B Lift-off at the same point at which the other aircraft lifted-off

C Lift-off at a point after the other aircraft lifted-off

D Wait 1 minute after the other aircraft has lifted-off and then lift-off at the same point as the other aircraft

99 Fuel pumps and many fuel filler caps are colour coded to alert pilots so they will not fill an aircraft with the wrong fuel. AVGAS filler points are colour coded:

A Black

B Green

C Brown

D Red

100 When flying within the UK for a private flight in an aircraft weighing less than 2400 kilograms, which documents must be carried and available for inspection?

A Pilot licence

B Radio licence

C Permit to Fly or Certificate of Airworthiness

D None

101 A Flight Plan must be filed for which of the following flights?

A A flight that crosses the UK international boundary

B A flight going more than 10 nautical miles from the coast

C A flight over sparsely populated areas

D A flight through an area where search and rescue operations are taking place

102 Other than aircraft taking-off and landing, which of the following has right of way over an aircraft taxying on the ground?

A A larger aircraft taxiing

B A vehicle

C A vehicle towing an aircraft

D A person

103 When more than one aircraft are approaching to land on the same runway, which has the right of way?

A The fastest aircraft

B The lowest aircraft

C The highest aircraft

D The nearest aircraft

104 When flying within the vicinity of an aerodrome which of the following is true?

A Aircraft should expect to make all turns to the left, unless signals or the existing traffic pattern indicates otherwise

B Aircraft must obey all instructions given by an Aerodrome Flight Information Service

C Aircraft must display lights to aid collision avoidance

D Gliders have priority over all other aircraft

Answers on page 170

Aerial Collision Avoidance

Aerial Collision Aviodance

- General Avoidance Regulations
- Converging
- Approaching Head-on
- Overtaking
- Right-hand Traffic Rule
- Airprox Reporting
- Revision

▶ General Avoidance Regulations

Regardless of any air traffic control clearance it is the duty of the commander of an aircraft to take all possible measures to see that he does not collide with any other aircraft.

- An aircraft must not fly so close to other aircraft as to create a danger of collision.
- Aircraft must not fly in formation unless the commanders have agreed to do so.
- An aircraft which is obliged to give way to another aircraft must avoid passing over or under or crossing ahead, unless passing well clear.
- An aircraft with right of way shall maintain its course and speed.
- For the purpose of this rule a glider and a machine towing it are considered to be a single aircraft under the command of the commander of the towing machine.

▶ Converging

Subject to the paragraphs below, an aircraft in the air must give way to other converging aircraft as follows:

- Flying machines must give way to airships, gliders and balloons.
- Airships must give way to gliders and balloons.
- Gliders must give way to balloons.

Subject to the above when two aircraft of the same type are converging at about the same altitude, the aircraft which has the other on its right must give way (normally by turning to the right).

- Powered aircraft must give way to those towing other aircraft or objects, such as banners.
- Foot launched powered flying machines must give way to all other aircraft.

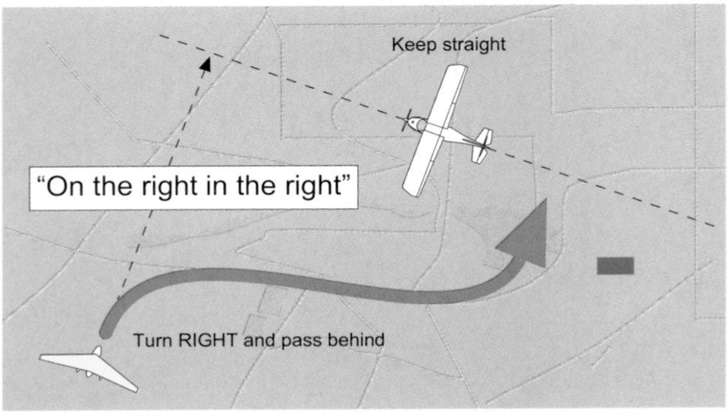

▶ Approaching Head-on

When two aircraft are approaching head-on, or nearly so, and there is danger of collision, each must turn right.

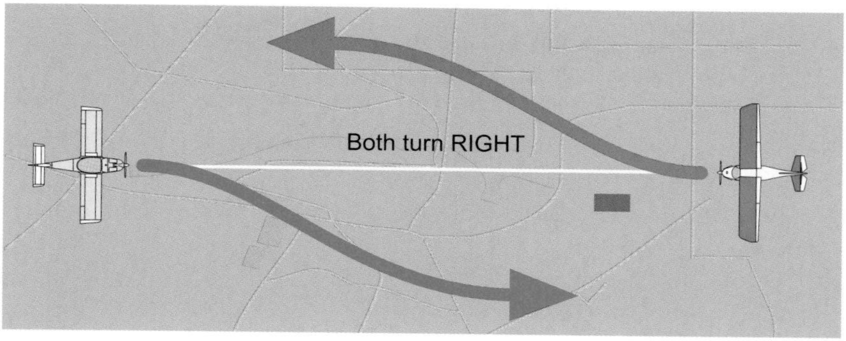

▶ Overtaking

An aircraft which is being overtaken in the air has right of way and the overtaking aircraft, whether climbing, descending or level, must keep out of the way by turning right.

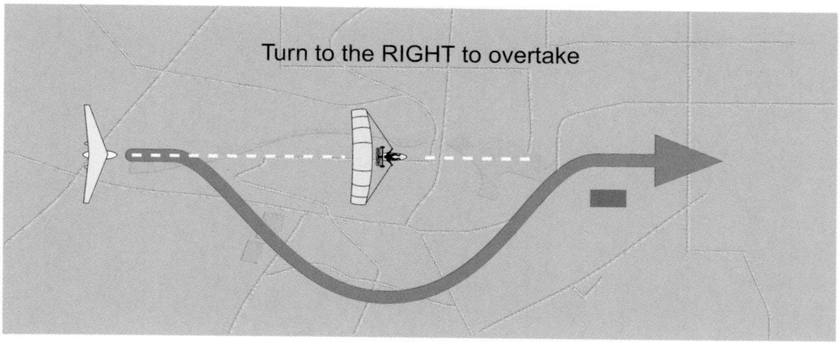

A glider overtaking another glider may, however, turn either right or left. This is to allow an overtaking glider to pass between the glider being overtaken and a ridge when hill soaring.

▶ Right-hand Traffic Rule

An aircraft flying in sight of the ground and following a road, railway, canal, coast or other line feature must keep that feature on its left except where it is instructed to do otherwise by the appropriate air traffic control authority.

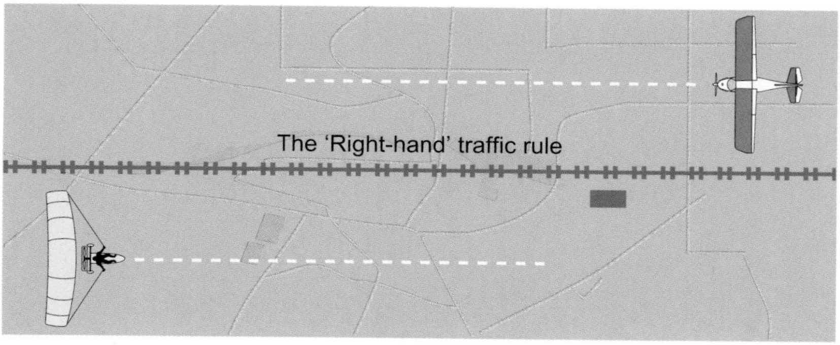

▶ Airprox Reporting

An Airprox has occurred when a pilot or controller considers that the distance between aircraft (together with their relative positions and speeds) has been such that the safety of the aircraft has been compromised.

An initial pilot report should be made by radio to the Air Traffic Service Unit, ATSU, with which the pilot is in communication with. If it is not possible to make an airprox report by radio, a report by telephone or any other means should be made as soon as possible after landing to any ATSU but preferably to an Area Control Centre (ACC).

Pilot reports made by radio or telephone must be confirmed within 7 days by completing the full AIRPROX reporting procedure.

Full details of the Airprox reporting procedure, and reports of investigations of reported Airproxs, can be found at: www.airproxboard.org.uk

▶ Revision

105 When two aircraft are approaching head-on or nearly so and there is a risk of collision:

A Both aircraft must turn around

B Both aircraft must turn left

C The faster aircraft should climb

D Both aircraft must turn right

106 A powered aircraft overtaking another powered aircraft in flight must do so by:

A Passing above the other

B Passing to the left of the other

C Passing to the right of the other

D Passing under the other

107 When following a line feature such as a railway line the aircraft must be flown to leave the line feature:

A Below

B To the right

C To the left

D To the left if heading North but to the right if heading South

108 In the event that you believe that you have flown so close to another aircraft that there was a risk of collision you should:

A Report the incident to an aerodrome in writing

B Report the incident to a radio service and follow up with a written report

C Report the incident to a radio service, there is no need for a written report

D Report the incident to the other pilot

Answers on page 170

Low Flying

Low Flying

- The Low Flying Rules
- Revision

▶The Low Flying Rules

500ft Rule

An aircraft must not fly closer than 500 feet to any person, vessel, vehicle or structure, except when landing and taking-off in accordance with normal aviation practice or when flying low for the purpose of dropping tow ropes, banners, etc at an aerodrome.

A glider is exempted from the 500 foot rule when hill soaring.

An aircraft practising approaches at a licensed aerodrome, in accordance with normal aviation practice, may fly within 500 feet of a person, vessel, vehicle or structure without contravening Rule 5.

An aircraft practising approaches at unlicensed aerodromes is not exempt from the 500 feet clearance required from a person, vessel, vehicle or structure. It is the pilot's responsibility to ensure that the required separation is maintained.

An inspection of a proposed landing area, such as a field site, may not be flown within 500 feet of a person, vessel, vehicle or structure.

Rule 5 makes it clear that flying within 500 feet of a person, vessel, vehicle or structure at anything other than a licensed airfield without landing is a breach of the Rule. However, an approach which has brought the aircraft within that distance should not be considered to be required to continue to a landing if the pilot considers that it would be unsafe to do so.

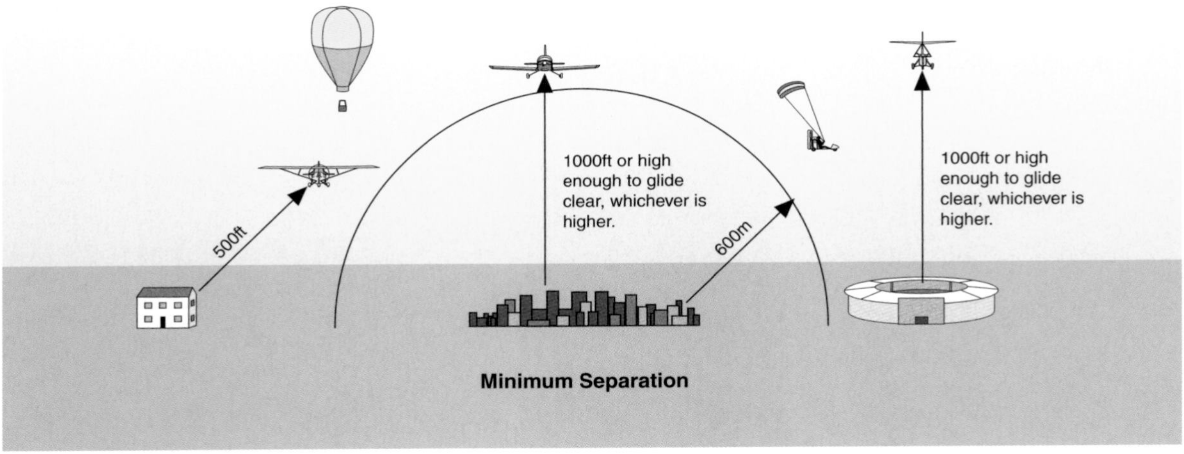

1000ft rule

An aircraft may not fly lower than 1000 feet over a gathering of 1000 people or more. It should be remembered that a microlight aircraft is in any case restricted by a condition of its Permit to Fly, which states that it may not fly over any assembly of people.

No aircraft shall fly below 1000 feet above the highest fixed object with a radius of 600 metres when flying over a congested area, unless taking-off or landing in accordance with normal aviation practice. No aircraft shall fly below a height that would allow it to make an emergency landing in the event of a power failure without causing danger to persons or property on the surface.

The restrictions on flights within 500 feet and below 1000 feet of gatherings of people do not apply when the flight is made at an air display or other such activity at which the people are attending and the aircraft is displaying in accordance with a display authorisation. The aircraft is not allowed to fly over the crowd.

Many aircraft operating on a Permit to Fly are further restricted concerning flying over built up areas (in addition to the 1000ft and 'glide clear' requirement). Always check the conditions of the permit for the type of aircraft that you are flying.

▶ Revision

109 Rule 5 of the Rules of the Air state that no aircraft shall fly closer than a certain distance from vehicles, persons, vessels and structures. That distance is:

A 100 feet

B 300 feet

C 500 feet

D 1000 feet

110 An aircraft may fly closer than the normal minimum when:

A Practising a landing approach at a private airfield where members of the public are not allowed

B Practising forced landing procedures over open countryside

C Practising a missed approach at a licensed aerodrome

D Inspecting a field when preparing for a precautionary landing

111 No powered aeroplane may fly over a built-up area:

A At a level below which, if the engine failed, it could not glide clear

B Below 1500 feet above the area even if approaching to land

C Unless the pilot has permission from air traffic control

D Without first filing a flight plan

Answers on page 170

Aerodrome Signals and Markings

Aerodrome Signals and Markings

- Aerodrome Markings
- Signal Area
- Signals
- Paved Runways and Taxiways
- Lights and Pyrotechnic Signals
- Misuse of Signals and Markings
- Marshalling Signals
- Revision

▶Aerodrome Markings

These rules detail the meaning of the standard signals and markings in use at UK aerodromes. It is an offence to use a signal for other than its prescribed meaning.

▶Signal Area

The signal area is a 12m square with white edges, visible from all directions. The area is normally situated close to the control tower or ATSU. Signals in the signal area can be seen by aircraft over-flying the aerodrome above 2000 feet and indicate the current aerodrome activity.

This area is at Kemble airfield. The letters 'KM' may help the pilot not quite sure of his or her actual position

▶Signals

Landing T

A white T in the signal area means that aeroplanes and gliders taking-off or landing must do so parallel with the shaft of the T and towards the cross arm unless otherwise authorised by air traffic control.

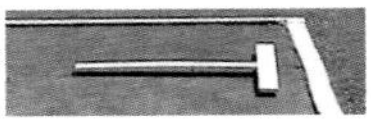

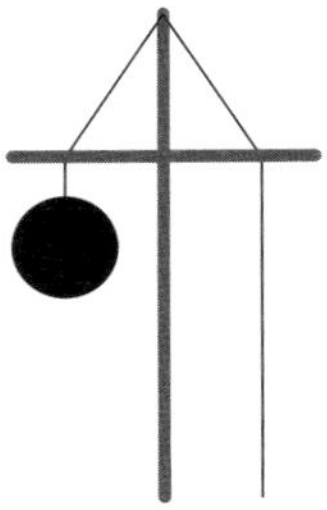

A white disk at the head of the T means that the direction of landing and direction of take-off do not necessarily coincide. The reason for this may be that the runway used for take-off is not the most suitable to use for landing in the prevailing conditions. An alternative signal displayed on a mast to near the signal area is a black ball suspended from the mast. The black ball would be visible to aircraft taxiing on the aerodrome.

White dumb-bell

A white dumb-bell means that aeroplanes and gliders on the ground are confined to paved, metalled or similar hard services.

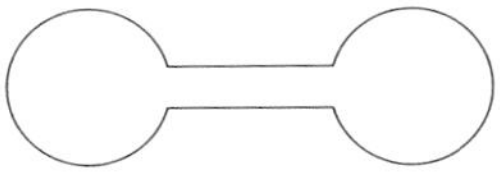

A black stripe on each circular part of the dumb-bell (at right angles to the shaft) means that aeroplanes and gliders taking-off or landing must do so on a paved runway but that movement on the ground is not confined to hard services.

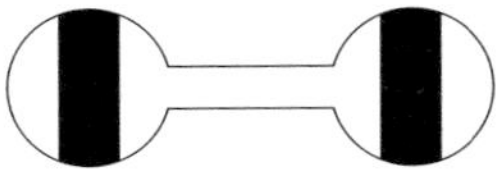

Light aircraft area

A red letter 'L' superimposed on the dumb-bell means that light aircraft are allowed to take-off and land either on a runway or on an area of the aerodrome designated by a white letter L.

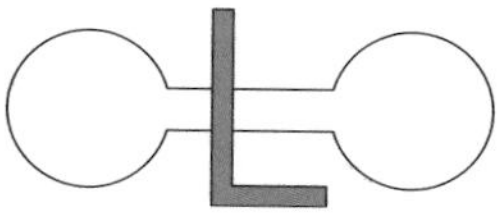

Right hand circuit

A red and yellow striped arrow turned through 90° around the edge of the signals area, and pointing in a clockwise direction, means that a right hand circuit is in force. An alternative signal is a green flag displayed on a mast near at the signal area, visible to aircraft taxiing on the aerodrome. If no signal is displayed it is assumed that a left hand circuit is in force.

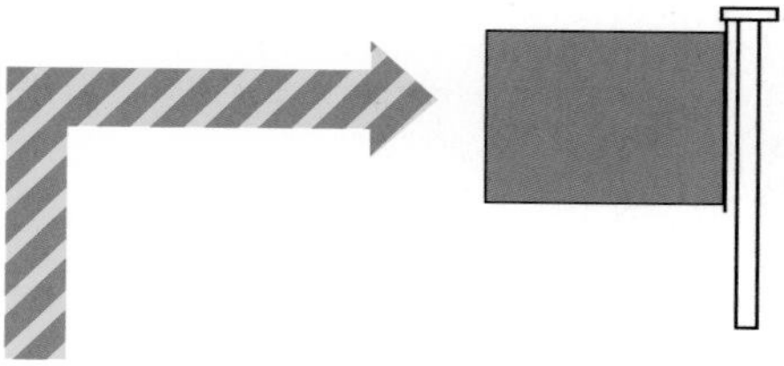

Special precautions

A red square with a single yellow diagonal stripe means that the state of the manoeuvring area is poor and that pilots must take special care when landing.

Landing prohibited

A red square with a yellow diagonal cross means that the aerodrome is unsafe for aircraft movements and that landing is prohibited.

Helicopter operations

A white H in the signals area means that helicopters must take-off and land only within a designated area. The designated area on the aerodrome will be marked by a much larger white H.

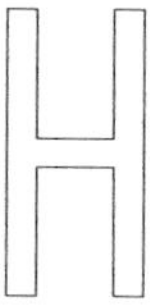

Gliding

A long white strip with two shorter strips across it, forming a double cross, means that gliding is taking place at the aerodrome. A similar but much larger signal is used to mark an area on the aerodrome which is to be used only by gliders. An alternative signal to indicate gliding in progress is 2 red balls suspended from the signals mast.

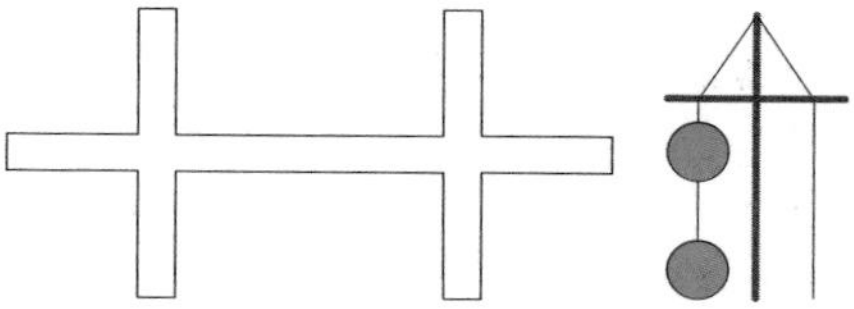

Control operations

A rectangular red and yellow chequered flag or board means that aircraft may move on the manoeuvring area and apron only with permission of air traffic control.

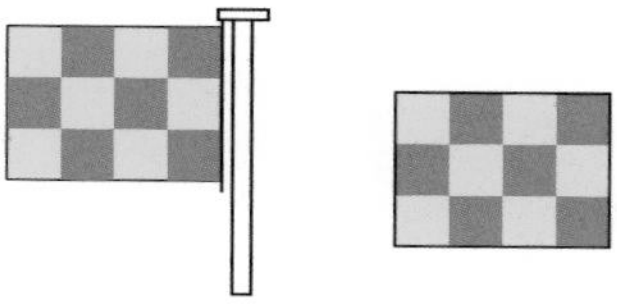

Reporting point

A square yellow board bearing a black letter C indicates the place at which a pilot can report to ATC or other aerodrome authority.

▶ Paved Runways and Taxiways

Unfit section of runway or taxiway

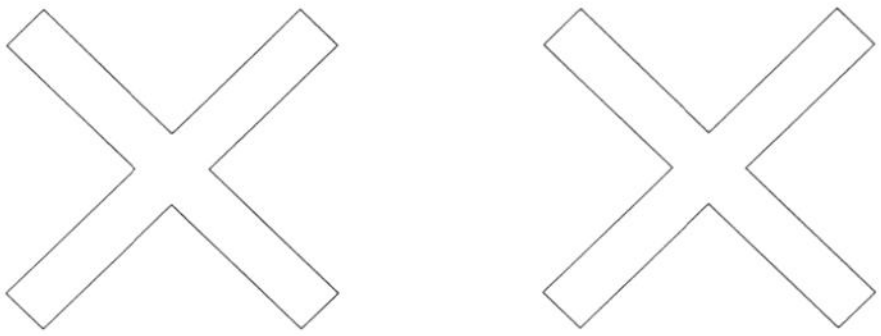

Two or more white crosses along a section of runway or taxiway, with the arms at 45° to the centreline, means that the section marked is unfit for the movement of aircraft.

Holding point

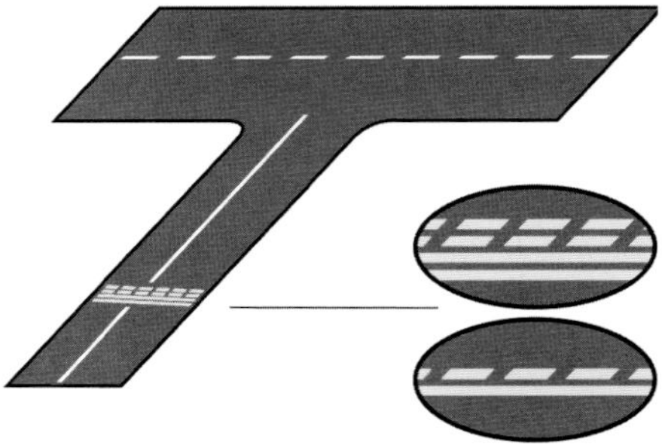

The holding point for a runway will be marked with a board showing the holding point reference and runway number. Two continuous yellow lines and two broken yellow lines across the taxiway also indicate a holding point, the broken lines will be on the runway side of the markings. Aircraft may cross the broken lines taxiing from the runway to the taxiway after landing without further permission. No part of the aircraft may cross the solid lines when taxiing to the runway without the permission of the aerodrome authority.

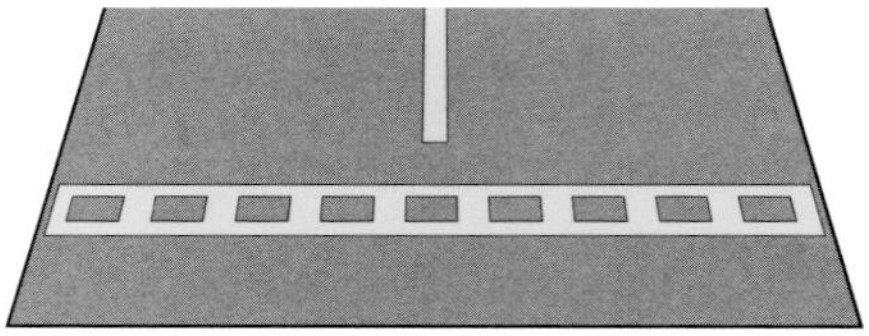

A yellow "ladder" marking across the taxiway marks a point that no aircraft may pass without the permission of ATC during the hours of watch of that unit.

Boundary of unfit paved areas

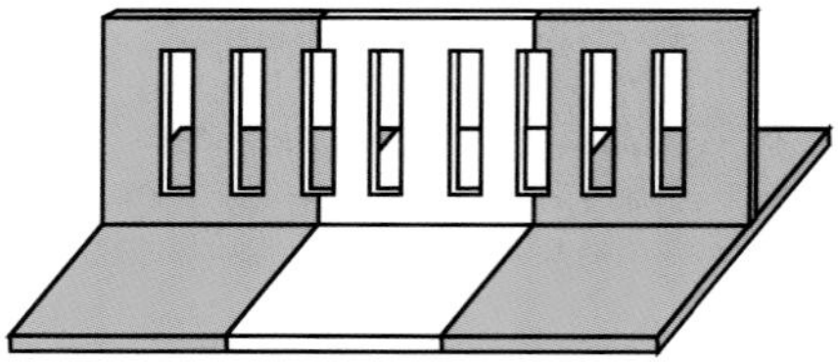

The boundary of any part of a runway, taxiway or apron which is unfit for aircraft movement is identified by orange/white markers. Each marker comprises a base board supporting a slatted vertical board, both striped orange – white – orange.

Unpaved runways and taxiways

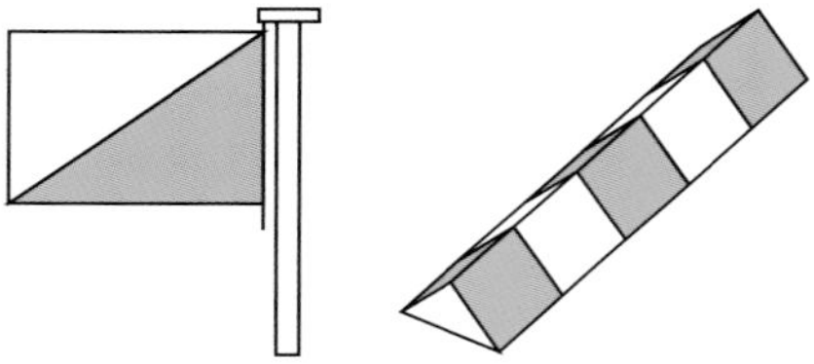

Boundary markers of unpaved runways and taxiways will be wedge shaped orange/white ground markers or orange/white flags.

Runway and stopway markers consist of 3 metre by 1 metre flat white markers flush with the ground.

▶ Lights and Pyrotechnic Signals

Light Signal	FROM AN AERODROME to Aircraft in Flight	FROM AN AERODROME to Aircraft on Ground
STEADY RED	Give way to other aircraft and continue circling	Stop
RED PYROTECHNIC LIGHT OR RED FLARE	Do not land; wait for permission	–
RED FLASHES	Do not land; aerodrome not available for landing	Move clear of landing area
GREEN FLASHES	Return to aerodrome; wait for permission to land	**To an aircraft:** You may move on the manoeuvring area and apron **To a vehicle:** you may move on the manoeuvring area
STEADY GREEN	You may land	You may take-off
WHITE FLASHES	Land at this aerodrome after receiving continuous green light and then, after receiving green flashes, proceed to apron	Return to starting point on the aerodrome

Light Signal	FROM AN AIRCRAFT IN FLIGHT TO AN ATSU
RED PYROTECHNIC LIGHT OR RED FLARE	Immediate assistance is requested
STEADY GREEN OR GREEN FLASHES OR GREEN PYROTECHNIC LIGHT OR GREEN FLARE	**By night:** May I land? **By day:** May I land in a direction different from that indicated from the landing T?
WHITE FLASHES OR WHITE PYROTECHNIC LIGHT OR SWITCHING ON AND OFF LANDING LIGHTS OR IRREGULAR FLASHING OF THE NAVIGATION LIGHTS	I am compelled to land

▶ Misuse of Signals and Markings

Signals and markings specified in the Rules with a particular meaning or for a particular purpose must not be used except with that meaning or for that purpose. Signals which maybe confused with a specified signal must not been made, and military signals must not be used, except with the necessary authority.

▶ Marshalling Signals

Meaning	Movement	In Daylight	By night
Proceed under the guidance of another marshal	Right or left arm down, the other arm moved across the body to indicate the position of another marshal		
Move ahead	Arms repeatedly moved up and back, beckoning onward.	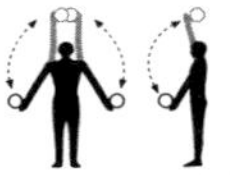	
Turn to Port	Right arm down, left up moved repeatedly up and back. The speed of movement indicates the rate of turn.		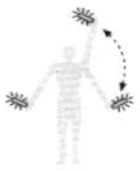
Turn to Starboard	Left arm down, right up moved repeatedly up and back. The speed of movement indicates the rate of turn.		
Stop	Arms repeatedly crossed above the head. The speed of movement indicates the urgency of the stop.		
Start engine	A circular movement of the right hand at head level with the left arm pointing to the engine.		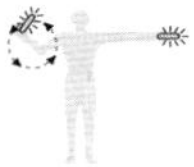
Chocks inserted	Arms outwards with the palms facing inwards and then swung inwards.	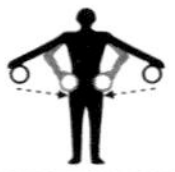	
Chocks away	Arms down with the palms facing outwards and then swung outwards.	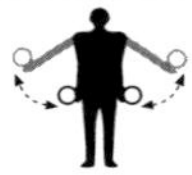	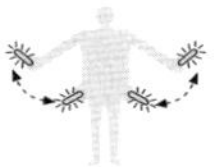
Cut engine	Either arm held level with the chest and then drawn across with the palm facing downwards.		
Slow down	Arms held down with the palms facing down and then moved up and down several times.		
This bay	Arms held above the head in a vertical position.		
All clear marshalling finished	Right arm raised at the elbow with the arm facing forwards.		

▶ Revision

112 In a signal square at an aerodrome the direction of landing and take-off is shown by:

A A dumbbell

B An arrow

C A white 'T'

D A white disc

113 Although you should always check before flight, at an airfield with a signal square if no ground signal indicates otherwise circuits are presumed to be:

A to the left

B to the right

C to the south

D to the outside of the airfield

114 A red square with a single yellow diagonal stripe across it displayed in the signal area means:

A That landing and take-off is prohibited

B The surface of the manoeuvring area is poor

C No left hand circuits are to be flown

D No right hand circuits are to be flown

115 A double white cross in the signals area shows:

A That gliding is taking place

B That there is a glider tow rope dropping area

C That parachuting is taking place

D That the aerodrome is closed

116 A black ball on a mast by the signal area means:

A the direction of take-off and landing are not necessarily the same

B a right hand circuit

C aerodrome closed

D no air traffic control is in operation

117 A continuous red light directed to an aircraft in the air by an air traffic controller means:

A Stop

B Give way to other aircraft and continue circling

C Do not land here

D Land with caution

118 White flashes from an aircraft in flight to the ground mean:

A "I am lost"

B "I am compelled to land"

C MAYDAY

D "May I land"

---

119 Arms of a marshal repeatedly crossed above the head means:

A Chocks away

B Move ahead

C Stop

D Chocks inserted

Answers on page 170

Distress, Difficulty and Urgency Signals

Distress, Difficulty and Urgency Signals

▶ Distress

The following signals, either together or separately before a message, mean that an aircraft is in grave and imminent danger and requires immediate help:

Radio call:	'Mayday Mayday Mayday.'
Visual signals:	SOS in Morse code (• • • – – – • • •)
	A succession of pyrotechnic single reds, fired at short intervals
	A red parachute flare
Sound signals, other than radio:	SOS in Morse code (• • • – – – • • •)
	A continuous sound with any apparatus
	Transponder setting of 7700
	Use of emergency radio frequency: 121.5MHz

▶ Difficulty

The following, either together or separately before a message, mean that an aircraft is in difficulties which compel it to land but it does not need immediate assistance:

A succession of white pyrotechnics

Repeated switching on and off of landing lights

Repeated switching on and off of navigation lights (in a manner distinguishable from normal flashing navigation lights)

▶ Urgency or Safety

The following, used either together or separately, mean that the aircraft has an urgent message to transmit concerning the safety of a ship, aircraft, vehicle; or other property; or of a person on board or within sight of the aircraft:

Radio call:	'Pan Pan, Pan Pan, Pan Pan'
Visual signals:	XXX in Morse code (– • • – – • • – – • • –)
Sound signals, other than radio:	XXX in Morse code (– • • – – • • – – • • –)

▶ Search and Rescue Signals

Survivors should use some or all of the following methods to attract attention when a search aircraft or surface craft is seen or heard:

- Fire distress flares or cartridges;
- Use some object with a bright flat surface as a heliograph;
- Flash a light;
- Fly anything in the form of a flag and, if possible, make the international distress signal by flying a ball, or something resembling a ball, below it;
- Blow whistles;
- Deploy fluorescent markers to leave a trail in the sea;
- Lay out air to ground visual signals as shown below as large as possible but at least 2·5 metres, 8 feet long.

▶ Ground Signals for Use by Survivors

Message	Code symbol
Require assistance	V
Require medical assistance	X
No or Negative	N
Yes or Affirm	Y
Proceeding in this direction	→

▶ Ground Signals for Use by Rescue Units

Message	Code symbol
Operation completed	LLL
We have found all personnel	LL
We have found only some personnel	++
We are not able to continue. Returning to base	X X
Have divided into two groups. Each proceeding in this direction	↗ ↘
Information received that the aircraft is in this direction	→ →
Nothing found. Will continue the search	N N

▶ Revision

120 An aircraft in distress should prefix the first radio call for help with the word:

A Pan Pan

B Tyro

C Help

D Mayday

121 An aircraft transmitting a call which contains information about another aircraft in difficulties should prefix the call with the word(s):

A Pan Pan

B Tyro

C Help

D Mayday

122 The ground signal from survivors of an aircraft accident to let a rescue party know they need medical assistance is:

A X

B V

C N

D Y

123 The ground signal made by a rescue party, to an aircraft, when they have completed their operation is:

A LL

B Y

C XXX

D LLL

Answers on page 171

Accident Investigation Regulations

Accident Investigation Regulations

- Accident Definition
- Revision

▶Accident Definition

An air accident is reportable if, between the time that anyone boards the aircraft with the intention of flight and such time as all have left the aircraft, any of the following happen:

- Anyone is killed or seriously injured while in or on the aircraft, or by direct contact with the aircraft or any part of the aircraft, except if the death or injury is self-inflicted or inflicted by another person, or if death is from natural causes.
- The aircraft suffers damage or structural failure other than damage limited to the engine and its accessories or minor damage to the aircraft structure.
- The aircraft is missing or completely inaccessible.

The report should be made by the commander, or if the commander is incapacitated, the operator, as soon as possible to the Chief Inspector of Air Accidents, the local Police Authority and in the case of a microlight aircraft to the Chief Safety Officer of the BMAA.

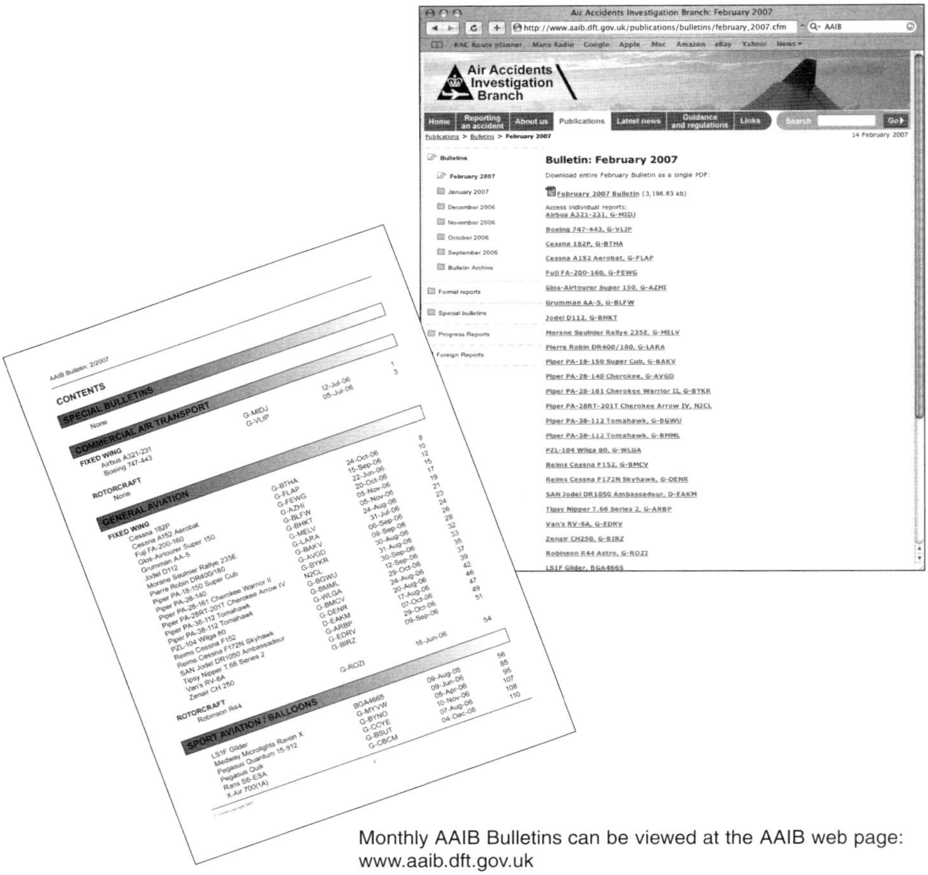

Monthly AAIB Bulletins can be viewed at the AAIB web page:
www.aaib.dft.gov.uk

▶ Revision

124 An Aircraft Accident is reportable if:

A It occurs to any aircraft at any time

B It occurs to commercial aircraft only, during a commercial flight

C It occurs to any aircraft between the time that the first person intending to fly in the aircraft boards and the last person disembarks after the flight

D If any damage, no matter how minor, occurs to the aircraft at any time other than during maintenance

125 Aircraft accidents should be reported to the:

A Chief Inspector of Air Accidents

B The CAA

C The Ministry of Transport

D The aircraft manufacturer

Answers on page 171

Revision Answers

Revision Answers

▶ Aeronautical Information

1 C

2 A

3 B

4 A

5 D

6 A

▶ Pilot Licencing

7 B

8 D

9 D

10 C

11 A

12 B

13 D

14 C

15 C

16 A

17 B

18 D

19 A

20 C

21 B

22 B

23 B

24 D

25 C

26 D

27 B

28 A

29 C

30 A

▶ Licence Considerations

31 D

32 A

33 D

34 D

35 B

36 C

37 A

▶ Instructor Ratings (Microlights) and Examiner Authorities

38 C

39 B

40 D

41 D

▶ Aircraft Registration and Airworthiness

42 C

43 B

44 B

45 D

46 D

▶ Aircraft Operation

47 C

48 A

49 A

50 B

51 B

52 C

53 D

54 A

▶ Visual Flight Rules (Rules 24-27)

55 A

56 C

▶ Airspace

57 C

58 D

59 A

60 A

61 C

62 D

63 A

64 C

65 D

66 A

67 C

68 A

69 C

▶ Airspace Restrictions and Hazards

70 B

71 C

72 D

73 B

74 D

75 B

76 A

77 D

78 A

79 D

80 C

81 D

82 C

83 B

84 C

▶ Royal Flights

85 A

▶ Air Traffic Services

86 C

87 A

88 D

▶ Altimeter Setting Procedures

89 A

90 D

91 B

92 D

93 C

▶ Operational Procedures and Rules of the Air

94 B

95 A

96 B

97 D

98 A

99 D

100 D

101 A

102 C

103 B

104 A

▶ Aerial Collision Avoidance

105 D

106 C

107 C

108 B

▶ Low Flying

109 C

110 C

111 A

▶ Aerodrome Signals and Markings

112 C

113 A

114 B

115 A

116 A

117 B

118 B

119 C

▶ Distress, Difficulty and Urgency signals

120 D

121 A

122 A

123 D

▶ Accident Investigation Regulations

124 C

125 A

Useful Contacts

Aeronautical Information Service
National Air Traffic Services Ltd
Control Tower Building
London Heathrow Airport
Hounslow
Middlesex
TW6 1JJ
Tel: 0208 7453450
www.ais.org.uk

Aircraft Accident Investigation
Department of Transport
Air Accidents Investigation Branch
Berkshire Copse Road
Aldershot
Hants
GU11 2HH
Tel: 01252 510300
www.aaib.gov.uk

Aircraft Owners and Pilots Association
50a Cambridge Street,
London
SW1V 4QQ
Tel: 0207 834 5631
www.aopa.co.uk

British Balloon and Airship Club
St John's Street
Bedminster
Bristol
BS3 4NH
Tel: 0117 953 1231
www.bbac.org

British Gliding Association
Kimberley House
Vaughan Way
Leicester
LE1 4SE
Tel: 0116 2531051
www.gliding.co.uk

British Hang Gliding and Paragliding Association
The Old Schoolroom
Loughborough Road
Leicester
LE4 5PJ
Tel: 0116 2611322
www.bhpa.co.uk

British Microlight Aircraft Association
Bullring
Deddington
Oxon
OX15 0TT
Tel: 01869 338888
www.bmaa.org

British Rotorcraft Association
532 Foundry Lane
Leeds
West Yorkshire L59 6RF
www.tonywilk.co.uk/bra/

Civil Aviation Authority
Aviation House
Gatwick Airport South
West Sussex
RH6 0YR
Tel: 01293 567171
www.caa co.uk

Helicopter Club of Great Britain
HCGB Secretary
Ryelands House
Aynho
Banbury
Oxon OX17 3AT
www.hcgb.co.uk

Popular Flying Association
Turweston Aerodrome
Nr Brackley
Northants
NN13 5YD
Tel: 01280 846 786
www.pfa.org.uk

List of Official Documents

Aeronautical Information Circulars (**AIC**)
Available via www.ais.org.uk

Aeronautical Information Publication (**AIP**)
Available via www.ais.org.uk

Air Navigation Order (**ANO**)
published by the Civil Aviation Authority as CAP 393.
Available via www.caa.co.uk

LASORS
published by the Civil Aviation Authority.
Available via www.caa.co.uk

NPPL Microlight Training Syllabus
Available from the British Microlight Aircraft Association

Index

M

N

O

P

Q

R

S